Thar She Blows

·R· MACEOV. Port Royal.

R· Grande.

A R· Belle.

R· de Gironde.

R· de Garonne.

R· de Charente.

R· de Loyre.

R· de Somme.

VIINA.

chiaca. R· de Seine.

R· de May.

Corine

SAVVRIONA.

R· des Daufins.

C· des François.

R

C· de Mort.

Thar She Blows

AMERICAN WHALING IN THE NINETEENTH CENTURY

STEPHEN CURRIE

LERNER PUBLICATIONS COMPANY • MINNEAPOLIS

This book is for Zubin, Kathryn, Josh, Corbett, Lacey, Morgan, Martin, Trevor, Talia, Emma, and Griffin, who sailed the oceans of the world with me in search of whales...

And for Amity, Irene, and Nick, who came as far as Mystic and New Bedford.

Lerner Publications Company
A division of Lerner Publishing Group
241 First Avenue North
Minneapolis, MN 55401 U.S.A.

Website address: www.lernerbooks.com

Library of Congress Cataloging-in-Publication Data

Currie, Stephen, 1960–
    Thar she blows: American whaling in the nineteenth century / by Stephen Currie.
        p.   cm. – (People's history)
        Includes bibliographical references and index.
        ISBN 0-8225-0646-7 (lib. bdg. : alk. paper)
        1. Whaling—United States—History—19th Century—Juvenile Literature. 2. Whalers (Persons)—United States—History—19th Century—Juvenile literature. [1. Whales. 2. Whaling.] I. Title. II. Series.
        SH383.2 .C87 2001
        639.2'8'0973—dc21   00–059489

Manufactured in the United States of America
1 2 3 4 5 6 – JR – 06 05 04 03 02 01

Contents

SHIPPING OUT

God knows I shall be glad when this cruise is ended. I would not suffer again as I have the last 3 months for all the Whales on the North West.
— Whaleman Joseph Eayrs, 1844

Eayrs's lament was a common one among the American men who went whaling in the nineteenth century. Although whaling involved travel to exotic islands and battling enormous creatures, whalers spent most of their time exhausted, bored, or terrified. Worse yet, voyages were long and the work was smelly, dirty, and dangerous. Whaling ships often did not return home for four or five years. "It's a rough, tough life full of toil and strife/We whalemen undergo," is the verse of a popular whaling song, and few whalers would have disagreed.

Why, then, did Americans hunt and kill whales? In a word, money. Whales were valuable. All whales have a layer of blubber, or fat, that helps protect them from cold water. Nineteenth-century American whalers were especially interested in sperm, right, and bowhead whales because these three species had a particularly thick layer of blubber. When melted down into liquid, the blubber became oil, which could be burned to provide light and heat. In nineteenth-century America, whale oil was one of the best sources of fuel available. Many households burned whale candles and whale lamps. The sperm whale also carried a supply of purer oil in its head. This high-grade oil was used to make expensive candles.

Whales were useful for other reasons, too. Right and bowhead whales were prized for their baleen. Commonly called "whalebone" by the whaling crews, baleen consists of hard yet flexible strips of cartilage that hang inside a whale's mouth. Whalebone helps the whale filter plankton and other tiny creatures out of the water. In the nineteenth century, strong, thin baleen was used to make fishing rods, buggy whips, and stays for corsets—the constricting undergarments that women wore around their waists to keep them fashionably small.

Opposite, *an illustration from Herman Melville's 1851 novel,* **Moby Dick** *which describes the perils of whaling in the nineteenth century. Above, whale oil was used for many products including machine oil.*

Whalers were also after ambergris—a pulpy, gray substance found in the stomachs of some sperm whales. Little is known about its biological purpose in whales. According to one theory, ambergris forms around things that whales swallow and cannot digest. Outside the whale, the substance was worth more than its weight in gold. Processed ambergris was added to perfume in very small amounts to keep the scent fresh and strong. Collecting enough ambergris could make a ship's owner very wealthy indeed.

The desire for light, beauty, and material goods all helped bring about the slaughter of whales. Products harvested from whales were in high demand until alternative sources became available in the late nineteenth century. Until then, catching and killing whales filled that need.

EARLY WHALERS

The first American whalers were Native Americans. They paddled canoes along the continent's northwestern and northeastern coasts in search of whales. Native American groups depended on whales for meat, fuel, and tools. Sailors from Europe began catching whales off the North American coast as early as the sixteenth century. These men from American ports sailed from early in the morning in 20-foot boats. They used rudimentary harpoons to spear the whales and then towed them back to shore for processing. The next day, the crew would go out again to hunt whales. While on the way to Plymouth Rock in 1620, the *Mayflower* stopped briefly in what would become Cape Cod Bay. According to one passenger, "we saw whales plying hard by us. If we had instruments and means to take them we might make a very rich return."

Over the years, however, the importance of whaling grew. Advances in technology helped whalers build ships that were specifically suited to hunting their prey. With more seaworthy vessels, increased storage space, and better navigational techniques, whalers moved away from the shorelines and into deeper waters. And as knowledge

Native Americans hammered stakes into the whale's blowhole, or nostril, and then attached a rope to the stake to tow the carcass ashore.

of the world grew, whalers moved from the familiar territory of the North American coasts into the distant waters of the Pacific and Indian Oceans.

By the 1800s, whaling had become a major industry that impacted the entire world. In addition to supplying people with fuel and other important goods, whaling brought people together and tore them apart. While at sea, whalers were separated from their families for months, even years. Those on the boats and those left behind formed their own unique communities. And as whaling ships sailed around the world in search of whales, whalers encountered different cultures. Whalers and the captains' wives who sometimes joined them on board are the ones who tell the history of whaling best. Through their journals, their letters, and their reminiscences, the whaling culture, the lands and peoples encountered, and the hardships whalers endured begin to take shape.

THE CREW

'Tis advertised in Boston,
New York, and Buffalo,
Five hundred brave Americans,
a-whaling for to go....
    —"Blow Ye Winds,"
    traditional whaling song

Whaling crews usually consisted of twenty-five to thirty-five men, often with very different backgrounds, experience, and responsibilities. A few were veterans of many whaling voyages, while others were on their first ocean trips. Crew members were white, black, Polynesian, and Native American. On every ship a handful of men gave the commands, and the rest followed their orders. On a four-year voyage on a small ship, these differences could lead to tension and even violence. In a way, the first and most important goal of the men aboard a whaling ship was to learn to tolerate each other's differences.

Responsibilities aboard whaling ships were carefully divided. Every man knew his rank and duties. The captain was in charge, and his word was law. Three or four mates, known as the ship's officers, assisted the captain. The harpooners, also known as boatsteerers,

Opposite, *crew members of the whale ship* **John R. Manta** *take a very brief break.* **Above,** *whalers in Kodiak, Alaska, pose with a 65-foot right whale.*

ranked below the mates. Usually there was one harpooner for each mate. The harpooners were junior officers. They had more responsibilities than ordinary sailors and earned more money, but they did not approach the status of the mates. The remaining fifteen to twenty sailors were called foremast hands. They gave no orders. Their jobs included steering the ship, standing watch, raising and lowering the anchor, and any other tasks their superior officers chose to give them.

Whaling ships also carried a few people whose responsibilities had nothing to do with the sea. They were officially called tradesmen, although envious crew members often spoke of them as "idlers" instead. The cooper provided and maintained the ship's casks and barrels. The carpenter kept the ship in good condition. The cook and the steward

James S. McKenzie was only fourteen when he took to the seas on board the whaling ship **Reindeer.**

cooked the meals. The cabin boy acted as the captain's personal servant. In the earliest days of whaling, before the nineteenth century, finding whaling crews was easy. Captains owned their own ships, and they advertised for crews by word of mouth. With few whaling ships and fewer ports, shortages of sailors were rare. Most captains had no problem filling their ships with local men. But as the whaling industry grew and voyages became longer, the situation began to change. More men were needed.

Recruiters, called shipping agents, advertised in newspapers and placed recruiting posters on trees and poles. "WHALEMEN WANTED," read an advertisement from 1839. "Experienced and Green Hands are wanted for the Ship's of the COLD SPRING WHALING COMPANY to sail from Cold Spring Harbor, Long Island." Agents also crisscrossed the Northeast in search of men who might be open to shipping on a whaler. Those who expressed interest were brought to the nearest port and signed up for a voyage. Even so, "Whaleships rarely leave home fully manned," explained Nathaniel Taylor, who sailed on the *Julius Caesar,* "but make it an object to procure men and boys, which they can do easily and cheaply, at some of the numerous islands in the Atlantic and Pacific Oceans."

ADVENTURE, MONEY, AND ESCAPE

Real whalers toured towns and cities talking about their lives. Some of these tours were made simply for entertainment purposes, while others were designed to recruit possible sailors. These speeches made an impression on some of the audience—a few signed up for an exciting journey of their own. "A Whaling Voyage Around the World!" read an advertisement for a lecture given by a New Hampshire captain. "All Hands Ahoy!" For many of those who decided to sail, the lure was adventure. "Gradually the idea came to me that I wanted to be a sailor," wrote one man about his boyhood, "and go to far distant lands, where giants, and cannibals, and naked savages, and other strange things exist, and of which I had read so much."

For others, the reason for sailing was economic. Although whaling made only a few sailors wealthy, many men hoped to be among those few. A diarist aboard the *Columbus* in 1852 wrote that the sailors all had "expectations of making a fortune in a short time." Some wanted to retire early. Others hoped to earn enough money to purchase land, open a store, or attract a wife. After his ship returned home, one crewman daydreamed, "there will be more marriages [taking] place and more farms bought than was Ever heard of before." For these men, whaling was all about making money.

A few men were less interested in getting rich than in surviving. They believed they had no alternatives to whaling. In his journal, sixteen-year-old Erastus Bills wrote, "My preference is to continue my studies, but I know I have no choice. I must get work that offers an immediate compensation. The only way open to me is seaward." Finally, some men went whaling because the life gave them a chance to escape. Criminals hiding from the law signed on for voyages that might last five years—this was an excellent way to avoid being put in jail. Others jumped aboard a whaling ship to escape family problems.

Whatever the reason, many whalers were not who they said they were. "It has become very fashionable for sailors to assume some fictitious name by which they ship," wrote one man in 1837. "By so doing many deprive their friends from tracing them." Many men, including at least two on the *Tiger*'s 1840 voyage, shipped under assumed names.

Young men, in particular, often ran away to go whaling. When Erastus Church was sixteen, his father sent him out to dig potatoes on the family farm. Mr. Church expected his son back by nightfall. Instead, Erastus did not come home for three years. Without telling anyone, he left the potatoes and ran off to join the crew of the *Phoenix*. Others did the same. An ad in a whaling newspaper offered a two-hundred-dollar reward for information about Edward B. Coe, believed to be on a whaler and wanted by his family urgently.

CHOOSING A CREW

During the mid-nineteenth century, agents began to have particular trouble finding men to sail. Ambitious and hardworking young men simply had better opportunities. Instead of taking to the seas, these would-be adventurers chose to enlist in the military or to head West to settle the new frontier. The pool of applicants dwindled to men who could find no other work or to men who were known troublemakers. "Too many ungovernable lads," complained a reporter for a Nantucket Island, Massachusetts, newspaper after surveying the sailors available for whaling jobs in 1836. "Too many vagabonds . . . too many convicts."

When there was a labor shortage, agents often resorted to deception to fill the ships. Agents downplayed the length of voyages, assuring recruits that the ships would fill up with oil in a matter of months. Agents often exaggerated the amount of money a sailor could make, too. "The wages," an agent advertised in a New Bedford, Massachusetts, newspaper, "are equal and in most cases superior to those in merchant ships." In truth, the regular wages paid by merchant ships were higher than the compensation for all but the luckiest whalers. More than one recruit sailed with great hopes, only to discover that the agent had misled him.

A few agents did more than just mislead. Two crewmen on the *Florence* were told that they were joining a fishing trip. They thought that they would be gone only a few days. A sailor on the *Tiger* said he had been kidnapped. "The shipping agent offered him a glass of grog & kept him drunk until night," a fellow crewman reported. When the sailor came to, he was already several miles out to sea. Stories like this were common during the nineteenth century, although not all the stories were entirely true.

When times were hard and few other jobs were available, agents could afford to be picky. In 1842, for instance, New Bedford was full of young men looking for work on a whaler. "The owners and [captains] were as difficult about pleasing as a lady buying a new dress," one sailor complained. At least one agent was known to ask for letters of reference, even from veteran seamen.

If there were plenty of applicants, a man's chance of being chosen depended partly on his size and health. Few agents signed up men who coughed or looked frail. Five-foot-tall Nelson Haley wanted to be a boatsteerer aboard the *Charles W. Morgan*, but the ship's owner was doubtful. "You look young and small for the position you would have to fill on board," he told Haley. But Haley got the job.

Sailors sometimes turned the tables and deceived the agents. Once out to sea, the captain of the *Tuscaloosa* discovered that many of his seamen were smaller than he had thought. The captain complained that one young recruit "must have had on several suits of clothes" when he applied for the job. "For several days he kept looking smaller & slim[m]er at last thinks I where will this all end. [H]ave we got the walking skeleton on board or not."

Men of all ages worked aboard whaling ships. The youngest crew during the nineteenth century belonged to the *Esquimaux;* those sailors averaged just seventeen years of age. However, many sailors were in their late twenties or beyond. Agents and shipowners took anyone willing to work for the pay they offered, whether those applicants had experience or not.

"GROWL YOU MAY BUT GO YOU MUST"

To join a crew, a sailor had to sign a contract called the ship's articles. The contract named the ship, the captain, and the port from which the ship would leave. The contract also specified a sailor's pay. Unlike most seamen, American whalers were not paid regular wages. Instead they signed on for a lay, or a portion of the catch. Typically, the captain got about one-tenth of the money earned from the voyage. A first mate might receive $1/18$ or $1/20$ of the total. The fractions dwindled from there. Fourth mates were entitled to about $1/60$, boatsteerers $1/80$, experienced seamen $1/150$, and greenhands as little as $1/200$. The rest of the catch belonged to the ships' owners.

Signing onto a whaling ship, therefore, was a gamble. A ship might earn so much that even the rawest greenhand would get a good share. The *Pioneer* arrived in New London, Connecticut, in 1865 with a catch worth more than $150,000. More than one captain was able to retire in comfort after only two or three voyages.

Still, the *Pioneer* was an exception. The system of lays probably hurt the sailors more often than it helped them. Luther Ripley's experience on the *Tiger* was common. "It is nearly 8 [months] since we left home," Ripley mourned at one point during his voyage, "and have only 120 bbls. [barrels] aboard. [M]y share would be about $20–2.50 per mo. in the best [years] of my life[.] [Too] horrible!! shameful!!!! [B]ut it cannot be helped. [G]rowl you may but go you must." Others fared even worse. Five months' work brought Richard Boyenton of the *Bengal* just six and a quarter cents.

RIGGING OUT THE CREW

Upon signing, a crew member received an advance on his pay, which would be deducted from his share at the end of the voyage. Next, he

Captain Benjamin A. Higgins was master of the whaling ship **Sunbeam.**

was sent to a waterfront supplier to be "rigged out," or properly equipped for the journey. A crewman would need warm clothes, gloves, blankets, jackknives, needles, thread, combs, and more. Some suppliers were honest, but too many sold poor quality merchandise at high prices. They were known to sailors as landsharks. By the time landsharks got through with a greenhorn, the advance was usually gone.

It was the agent's job to get the crewmen on board ship. This was not always easy. Because crew members trickled in over a period of days, the earliest to join had time to change their minds before sailing, and about one in five did. Some took offers from other ships instead. Others, upon seeing the ship that would be their home for the next several years, decided that they had made a dreadful mistake. Four-year voyages, cramped quarters, and seasickness were not for them. Those who backed out of their commitments created a problem for shipowners and agents alike. The agent forfeited his bounty of five or ten dollars per recruit, and the owners usually lost money paid in advance.

When slavery was still practiced in the South and racial prejudice was rampant, whaling was one of the few industries that hired African Americans.

PREJUDICE ON BOARD

From its earliest days, American whaling was a multicultural affair. Hawaiians hauled up the anchor beside American blacks and Portuguese-speaking Cape Verdeans. Before the nineteenth century, captains frequently hired Native Americans as crewmen. Later, free African Americans came to the whaling towns along the Atlantic coast. The *Industry,* which sailed in 1822, had an all-black crew. These men were drawn to the whaling business because it was more tolerant of African Americans than were most industries of the time. Shipowners paid black sailors close to what white sailors received and hired men with little regard to their race. A few African American men even rose to the status of captain.

But the industry's commitment to hiring black sailors did not always mean white shipmates treated them with respect. Racial prejudice was everywhere—in the living quarters, in the whaling boats, among captains. On the *Rambler*, white seamen slept in one room, blacks in another. Some observers claimed that captains mistreated African American sailors toward the end of a voyage, hoping that the men would leave the ship and not collect their pay. "An African is treated like a brute by the officers of these [whaling] ships," summed up one white Nantucket sailor.

Men from two foreign groups were especially likely to sign on to an American whaling ship. The first included dark-skinned men from the Azores and the Cape Verde Islands, Atlantic ports belonging to Portugal. Known among whalers as Portuguese or simply "Gees," Azoreans and Cape Verdeans came from a long seafaring tradition. Polynesian sailors from various Pacific islands made up the second group. Americans called them Kanakas, which is a Hawaiian word for "person." The *Addison* had at least seven Azoreans when she left New Bedford in 1856. Later in her four-year voyage, she picked up many more Azoreans and at least twenty-six Hawaiian crewmen.

In general, officers treated white American sailors with more respect than they did men of other races. Especially in the Pacific, most ships paid foreign sailors in wages rather than lays. Peruvian sailors were usually given $15 a month, for example. In some cases, if the voyage was relatively unsuccessful, the money was fair and hired hands actually earned more than American sailors. In most cases, however, the salary failed to match even the meager earnings of American sailors.

Most white men did not bother to get to know the foreigners well. White Americans sometimes resented the "jabbering" of the foreigners in their own languages or the differences in dress, customs, or temperament. Some American sailors were downright cruel. When a Cape Verdean died aboard the *South Boston*, Samuel Morgan noted that the crew "would have felt worse had he not been a Portugee." Nevertheless, crew members did have to work with everyone else on board the ship. Often, this was the first time these men had met people from other cultures and backgrounds, since Americans of this era rarely traveled far from home.

THE VOYAGE

The lookout in the cross-trees stood,
With a spyglass in his hand.
"There's a whale, there's a whale,
there's a whalefish," he cried,
"And she blows at every span,
brave boys,
And she blows at every span."
— "Greenland Whale Fisheries,"
    traditional whaling song

Nearly all whaling ships set sail from various ports throughout the northeastern United States. Until the early nineteenth century, most ships came from Nantucket, Massachusetts. Later on, it was more common for ships to sail from the mainland city of New Bedford, Massachusetts. Other popular ports included New London, Connecticut, and Cold Spring Harbor, New York. A handful of ships sailed from San Francisco, California, especially toward the end of the nineteenth century. Ships even sailed from Hudson, New York, a river port located more than one hundred miles from the ocean.

Once out of port, the barrel-shaped whaling ships plodded along. Boxy and solid, the ships were very slow. "You could have shifted the sails around and sailed her stern first," a seaman once scoffed, "and she would have gone just as well." But then, whaling ships were not built to look good or to win races. Instead, they were designed to provide a lot of cargo space. Captains needed to store as much whale oil as possible. Every nineteenth-century whaling ship had a large hold, often at the expense of working and living areas.

THE SEARCH

Finding whales was not easy. Although nineteenth-century captains often had good information about whales and their habits, they could not know precisely where whales would be at any given time. Hunting for whales, then, involved plenty of guesswork. Many whalers covered much of the globe in search of whales. A few nineteenth-century ships forged into the northern Atlantic Ocean, near Greenland. More rounded Cape Horn, the southernmost tip of South America, and hunted in the Pacific Ocean off the western coast of Peru. Still others set sail for the Indian Ocean, for the South Atlantic, for Japan, for Hawaii, or for the Bering Sea.

Looking out for whales was a scary job. Crew members took turns stationing themselves in the ship's crosstrees, two horizontal supports located near the top of the mast. To reach the crosstrees, whalers had to climb the ship's rigging and sometimes even inch their way across beams, trying to keep their balance 50 feet up while big waves and strong winds rocked the ship. Once in the crosstrees, crewmen would have to ignore the pitching of the ship and scan the horizon, searching for whales.

Sailors did not enjoy lookout duty. The job was lonely, and the crosstrees were open to wind, rain, and cold. The work required keen eyesight and excellent concentration. Captains sometimes offered a prize to the crewman who saw the first whale. On one voyage of the *Kathleen*, for instance, the captain promised five dollars for the first sighting. Other captains offered different rewards, such as tobacco and a pig aboard the *Tiger*, or sausage cakes and a bottle of beer on the *Kingsdown*.

Sometimes the lookout was lucky and whales would surface near the ship, making identification easy. Most of the time, however, the first sign of a whale was small and easy to miss: the flash of a fin or tail in the distance, a waterspout, even a dark smudge against the waves. With experience, a lookout became adept at reading the signs and seeing whales, even at great distances.

When the lookout was reasonably sure he had seen a whale, he would shout to alert the sailors on the deck below. Some lookouts yelled "Thar she blows!" although other common cries included "There goes flukes [tail fins]!" or simply "Thar blows!" The typical response from the captain was "Where away? How many? And how far off?" The lookout then replied with the position, number, and distance of what he had seen.

In the meantime, eager sailors would crowd the deck. "There is nothing so electrifying as that cry from the masthead," William Fish Williams reminisced years after his last voyage. Few men forgot their first glimpse of whales. "Everyone was on the alert," wrote Nathaniel Taylor. "The creature was in plain sight, one moment spouting and rushing rapidly through the surface, and the next diving into depths unknown, throwing his flukes high in midair as he went down." Nelson Haley's first sighting was of whales "tumbling about" in the water. "I have never seen whales at play before or since," he said afterward. "It seemed too bad to interrupt their pastime, but they were the fish we had crossed three oceans [and] into the fourth to find."

Occasionally, a captain would choose not to chase after whales. If darkness were near, if the whales were small and far away, or if the crew were sick and hungry, he might decide to leave the whales alone. Usually, however, captains ordered the crew to lower the small vessels called whaleboats and head out after the whale. The chase was on.

LOWERING THE BOATS

Whaleboats were low and sleek, 24 feet long, but with bottoms only half an inch thick. Whaling ships usually carried three to five whaleboats. The boats hung above the ship's deck, already loaded with food, water, rope, axes, harpoons, and other tools. A well-rehearsed crew could lower the boats over the edge and into the water, get in, and be under way "in a twinkling," as one seaman put it. The crews did move fast. "Every man seemed to be a part of some vast machine," wrote Nathaniel Taylor, "so quickly was the ship trimmed for pursuit and the boats put in readiness for lowering." Depending on the distance and the number of whales spotted, only one whaleboat, or all five, might be lowered.

Each boat included a crew of six: the captain or a mate, a harpooner, and four foremast hands. The officer stood in the stern, or back of the boat, steering with a long oar. The harpooner took the

The six crewmen in the whaleboat had a tough time following a whale through the waves.

oar closest to the bow, or front. The other men rowed, too. If the crew was lucky and the whale was downwind of the ship, they could use sails instead. Though the men tried to go quickly, they knew their limits. If they tried to go too fast, they might gally, or scare, the whale, causing it to swim away. No whaleboat could catch up with a whale at high speed.

Throughout the chase, the officers kept a close eye on their prey. If the whale dove, veteran whalers could often predict where and when it would resurface. The crew got help, too, from those who remained behind. "On board the Ship," wrote Eliza Williams:

> they place signals to [the] mast head in different places, and different shaped ones, made from blue and white cloth, to let those in the boats know in what direction the whales are and whether they are up or down, as it is difficult for the Men in the boats to tell, they are so low on the water and the whales change their positions so often.

The exact arrangement of flags and their meanings varied from ship to ship. A standard code would have told competing nearby ships the location of the whale as well.

The chase was exhausting, and the exhaustion seemed worse when the whales got away. "The whales are up," wrote Robert Weir aboard the *Clara Bell:*

> We see them from the boat—off we put—gain on them fast—get about three ships length when they lift their flukes and sound [dive] again—After having an exciting chase of three, four, or more hours we turn about and go on board disheartened—tired & disgusted—such is the sad history of the first whale we saw, chased & didn't get.

Crews often spent four or more hours chasing a whale. A whale led the *Hannibal's* boats 50 miles away from the ship once, only to escape. "Landsmen," wrote crewman Nathaniel Morgan, "who think the life of a whaleman all fun and nothing to do, had better try a pull or two of this kind and then judge."

STRIKE!

Ideally, a boat would catch up to a whale and be nearly on top of it when it spanned, or surfaced to breathe. If the crew were close enough, the mate would then direct the harpooner to strike at the whale with the harpoons. Until the end of the 1800s, when close-range harpoon guns were developed, the harpoons had to be driven into the whale by hand. It was a dramatic and frightening experience to be so close to such a large animal. "I was up in a moment," wrote Robert Weir, "picked up my first iron and darted with Might and Main right in the center of Leviathan's [the whale's] side—the second harpoon was buried in the bunch of his neck."

The harpoon itself consisted of two parts: a long wooden handle and a point made of iron, with a hook at the end to keep it from falling out of the whale's flesh. The handle was attached to a coil of rope hundreds of yards long. The rope was essential because harpoons did not kill the whales. Instead, harpoons only weakened and maddened them. The rope kept the boat connected to the prey.

Even after the whale was harpooned, crews usually prepared for a chase that might last two or more hours. Assuming all went well, the whale would soon become exhausted from struggling against the rope. It would also grow weak from loss of blood. With patience, strength, and luck, the whalers could outlast the whale. Little by little the crew wound up the rope—sometimes actually pulling the boat onto the whale's back.

But all didn't always go as planned. Some whales would run, or swim as fast as possible along the surface or just below it, dragging the boat behind. Whalers called this a "Nantucket sleigh ride." Nathaniel Taylor once watched a boat from the whaler *Marcia* being dragged in this way. He called the boat a "mere egg-shell . . . so

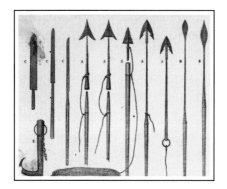

Harpoons had wood handles and iron points. Attached was a long rope that connected the boat to a harpooned whale.

swiftly borne along by the angry monster of the deep that it seemed barely to touch the top of each successive wave." Nantucket sleigh rides were certainly exciting. They could also be dangerous. "Some of these whales have a smart run," observed Almira Gibbs. "I think I should not like to be in the boats when they are fast to a smart fish."

Other whales would sound, or dive swiftly toward the bottom. Many minutes could go by before these whales spanned again. In this case, the crew had to watch the rope carefully. If the whale descended too low, a crewman would cut the rope with an ax rather than risk having the boat pulled underwater. Losing the whale was preferable to losing the whaleboat. Crewmen also had to be careful to stay clear of the rope, which uncoiled at high speeds. Captain Martin Palmer of the *Kingfisher* was one of many who did not. Palmer "got fast in the line," reported Eliza Williams, "and was taken down by the whale and never seen again."

More dangerous, though, were the whales that went into a frenzy right on the surface. Whaleboat crews tried to get as far as possible from the whale after hooking it, but it was not always clear in which direction the animal would move. Many men were struck by a fin or a twitching tail and injured. "Jonathan got swept overboard by the whale and hurt badly," wrote a diarist aboard the *Emma C. Jones.*

Sometimes the whale attacked the small, flimsy whaleboats. An angry and injured whale had tremendous power and strength. Whales stove, or smashed, many boats. "A boat was towed to the *Catharine* very badly stoven," read a diary entry from 1847. "One man was so injured it is not supposed he can live through the night. Another poor man was never seen after the whale struck the boat. [H]e must have been killed by the whale." Under the right circumstances, whales could destroy even a large whaling ship: the *Kathleen* and the *Essex* were among those suffering that fate. The *Essex* was destroyed by an 85-foot-long sperm whale that had swum at the ship as it sailed between the Galápagos and Marquesas Islands in the Pacific Ocean. First the whale struck the side of the ship. The crew members chose not to spear it, thinking it would try to destroy the rudder. But the whale swam back, hitting the front of the ship and sinking it. The crewmen climbed into one of the whaleboats and saved what they could from the *Essex*. The men thought that the whale had destroyed the boat deliberately: "His aspect was most horrible, and as such indicated resentment and fury," one reported afterward. Whaleboat

Harpooners had the difficult task of ramming the sharp tip of a harpoon into the thick skin of a swimming whale.

crews were well aware of the dangers but could do little to prevent a stoven boat if the whale should happen to attack.

"RED WITH THE BLOOD OF THE WHALE"

When the whale finally tired, it was time to move in for the kill. In the early days of whaling, the mate would go to the bow of the ship and stab the whale with a lance, a weapon much like a spear. He aimed the lance just behind the whale's neck, where the arteries met the lungs. "We soon haul close," wrote Robert Weir, "and the Mate has darted the lance chock to the socket in Leviathan's very vitals—again the water foams—but this time it is red with the blood of the whale." The officer struck at the same spot repeatedly until the whale drowned. By the 1850s, however, it was more common to use "bomb-guns," which could fire the lances from a distance.

Once the whale was finally dead, or "fin up" as the whalers put it, the crew had to tow the dead whale back to the ship. This was hard and backbreaking work. The bloody whale carcass also attracted sharks and other scavengers, which made the job even worse. Whalers used their oars to ward off sharks. Bringing in the whale was especially grueling if the chase had taken the boat out of sight of the ship. In such cases, the crew would just head in the general direction of the whaler and hope for the best. With or without whales, many whaleboat crews got lost and spent an anxious night, or even several days, searching for their ship.

CUTTING IN AND TRYING OUT

Back at the ship, whalers prepared for the messy job of cutting in—cutting the whale into pieces to extract the whalebone, ambergris, and barrels of oil. It would have taken too much time to haul each whale back to shore for the cutting in, so whalers cut up the whales on the ship.

To cut the blubber from the whale, sailors worked together using chains and a crank to hoist the carcass alongside the ship, above the water and just below the deck. Next, a few men sawed the head off the whale, a messy task that often took hours.

If the whale were a sperm, the head was especially valuable. It might contain as much as thirty barrels of oil. Reaching this oil, however, was no job for the squeamish. Sailors used ropes and pulleys to drag the head close to the deck or, if the head was small enough, up onto the deck. Then the crew used knives to create a gaping hole in the top of the skull. The work was hard and bloody, but it was the only way to reach the oil, which was located inside the skull. Sometimes the men could reach up with buckets and skim some of the oil off the surface, but more often sailors simply climbed into the oily mass. "[We] hoisted her head about two feet above water," wrote the proud captain of the *Grampus*, "and a man got in up to his armpits and dipped out almost 6 hogsheads of clear oil." The sight was repeated on other ships. "Wouldn't this be a rich scene for the dear ones at home to see," commented Robert Weir. "A couple of men burried in a whale head—a delightful situation surely."

Once the head was off, the crew cut up the rest of the body. Sailors used a rope to lower one of the boatsteerers onto the whale's back, where he pierced the skin with an enormous tool called a blubber hook. "It is no easy task to haul a hook that will weigh about one hundred and twenty pounds some fifteen or twenty feet out from the side of the ship and turn the hook, point out, in the hole," Nelson Haley explained, "taking into consideration that you are all the time clinging like a crab to keep yourself on the whale's back." Not only was the footing slippery at best, but the whale pitched and rolled as the boat was tossed by the waves and the current. Sharks swam nearby, too. The boatsteerer's only comfort was the rope that connected him to the ship.

The cut exposed the blubber, the layer of fat just underneath the skin. On a large whale, the blubber could be nearly two feet thick. The crew then had to cut the blubber away from the bones. Starting with the hole made by the blubber hook, sailors peeled off the blubber in spiral strips, turning the whale as they did so. The men hoisted the strips over the side of the boat.

Cutting in was dangerous work. Men lost their balance on the slippery decks. Some fell overboard or broke legs. On the *Lydia*, a man lost his big toe when he dropped a cask full of oil on his foot. On another vessel, a crewman's hand became trapped between the whale and the side of the ship. Several of the man's fingers split open, "one of them most sadly," his captain reported.

The big pieces of blubber were hard to move around. "We would cut off a blanket piece [a section of blubber] and hoist it," remembered a crewman on the *Kathleen*, "but before we could lower it into the blubber room it would go swinging across the deck in all directions." During one cutting in, a piece of blubber fell on the captain of the *Ontario* and killed him. On the *Louisa*, the jaw of a whale narrowly missed two crewmen. "I stay in the [cabin]," wrote a captain's wife, "and watch proceedings ofttimes holding my breath at the apparent danger."

Eventually, the crew would haul the blubber to a room below decks, where they cut the strips into smaller, more workable chunks. Whaling ships, then, were also floating factories.

As the ships sailed, crews built large brick stoves called tryworks on the decks. Crew members brought the chunks back to the deck and dropped them into the try-pots—large kettles placed over the fire in the tryworks. The heat of the fire gradually boiled the blubber down into oil. The hot oil caused many injuries, too. "We were boilling a whale," wrote John Deblois to his wife, "a Cask had a bout 2 bbls of scalding oil in it, it bursted and the hot oil came all over me every bodday thought that I shold be a criple for life."

The process was grimy and greasy and smelly. The decks were covered with oil and piles of blubber. Grease clung to the men's hands and stuck in their hair. Thick black smoke from the tryworks belched into the sky. The rotting whale and the heating blubber stank. "The odor from a whaling ship is horribly offensive," wrote one observer.

Crews peeled off blubber in spiral strips while the whale carcass was still in the water beside the ship.

Nathaniel Taylor complained that the smell of the smoke "penetrates every corner." The men worked around the clock. "You start cutting in," remembered a whaler, "and you don't stop no 12 o'clock, no one o'clock for dinner, you keep going until you cut that entire whale in and then you can eat again."

In the end, the blubber was reduced to liquid fat, cooled, and stored in wooden casks in the hold. The sailors stored away whalebone, ambergris, and any other useful material as well. Sometimes the crew ate whale steaks for a few days. Finally, the crew swabbed down the decks and prepared for the next whale. "The work is very greasy as well as very hard," wrote one diarist in 1867, "and I should say that it is only the thought of the money that is expected that makes it endurable."

BROKEN VOYAGES

The money, however, was still a long way off. Few captains wanted to return home before filling their holds with oil. Ships that returned less than full were scorned as having made "broken voyages." In contrast, captains whose ships overflowed with oil were applauded upon their return. The *Loper* went down into legend by returning to Nantucket with its deck and its hold both crammed with casks. The captain of the *Brewster* threw food and water overboard to make room for more oil. In 1859 a handful of ships came upon a large pod of whales in the Bering Sea. The *Mary and Susan* alone processed 1,600 barrels in less than a month, filling about half its available space.

Such ships were unusually successful, but other captains held up these experiences as examples to the crew. To give up too early would damage the captain's reputation. "If I live to reach home," wrote Leonard Gifford of the *Hope*, "no man shall be able to say by me thear goes a fellow that brought home a broken voyage."

Indeed, captains in the Pacific were so anxious to do well that they sometimes chose to continue whaling even after the ship was full. Rather than making a long trip around Cape Horn, dropping off their oil in New England, and then returning to the hunting grounds, they paid other captains to bring the oil back to New England for them. The *Nile* took this strategy to the limit. That ship left New London in 1859 and regularly sent oil home but did not itself return for eleven years.

By the middle of the nineteenth century, very few ships were staying out for less than a year. By the time a ship reached a whaling ground, killed the necessary number of whales to fill its hold with oil, and made the long voyage home, two to four years had usually passed.

As ships crisscrossed the oceans, their prey often eluded them. In the early years of whaling, the main problem was one of timing. A bay that had been full of whales one day might not be so a year, a month, or even a week later. "We got here a little too late," wrote a diarist aboard the *Florida* in 1858. "The Ships that were here a few days ago got a nice cut of Oil—some of them 600 bbls. The Whales were plenty. They have left now."

Later on, the combination of overhunting and changes in the habits of whales often made searching slow and frustrating. Many whalers would have identified with the diarist who wrote, "Week after week passes away and no whales."

HOMEWARD BOUND

At some point, the captain of the ship would decide to head for home. Ideally, the end came as soon as the ship was filled with barrels of oil. In some cases, however, months of unsuccessful searching made captains eager to cut their losses and start afresh, even if doing so meant returning home a broken voyage.

On the return trip, the crew did not usually pursue whales. In fact, most crews ensured that their ship would catch no more. Sailors often dismantled the tryworks and ceremoniously tossed the bricks into the ocean, making it impossible to render more blubber into oil. "The masonry composing the tryworks was torn down," reported Nathaniel Taylor in February 1853, when the *Julius Caesar* was still near Antarctica. "The heavy iron try-pots were launched into the ocean, the decks cleaned and the ship put in order for her passage home." His ship docked in New London that June.

Once the try-pots were gone, the end had arrived. All that was left was cleaning the ship and sailing home as fast as possible. Crewmen could hope for a good catch and a good price on the oil they had collected. They could do nothing more.

"EXHAUSTED BODY AND BLISTERED HANDS"

'Tis there we'll cruise a month or
two and never see a whale;
Our water all stagnated grows,
And our provisions fail.
    — "Old Nantucket,"
    traditional whaling song

Whaling ships often went for weeks without seeing a single whale. As a result, most of the crewmen's time was spent doing routine tasks. It was true that few jobs were as exciting and dramatic as whaling once a whale had been sighted—but it was also true that few jobs were as dull during the remaining parts of the voyage.

Shortage of work was never a problem. Sailors scrubbed the decks, spliced rope, tested the whaleboats, and hauled the sails up and down. Men rotated the watch, so at least a few sailors were always on the lookout for whales. At times the routine felt like busywork. "At four o'clock the mate said that we had better wash decks," one man reported. "I thought to myself that they had had enough washing to last the voyage, but orders is orders." Whatever the task, it took a toll on the crew. "Tumbled into my bunk with exhausted body and blistered hands," wrote a greenhand.

SLEEPING QUARTERS

Ordinary seamen slept below decks in a room called the forecastle. The forecastle was small—twelve feet by twelve feet in some ships— with a low ceiling. With more than a dozen men, it was unimaginably crowded. Men slept in bunks so close together that one man's feet were practically in his neighbor's face. On most whalers there was not even room for each man to have his own bunk. So the men had to sleep in shifts. The close quarters were a problem for many whalers. "It is the confinement that I hate," Will Woods wrote soon after setting sail.

The tight sleeping quarters seemed even smaller when one of the men got sick. Most sailors had trouble adjusting to the ocean, and seasickness was widespread during the early parts of the voyage. "Was taken sea sick," a *Hannibal* crewman wrote. "Discharged my dinner very readily." Even the gentlest breeze could set the ship to rocking; it didn't take much motion to nauseate those accustomed to solid ground. In the middle of a hunt or a cutting in, all men had to work, even if they were sick. "And oh! how dreadfully sick I was!" Robert Weir moaned. "Saw two sharks . . . I felt very much tempted to throw myself to them for food."

Officers had somewhat better quarters. The mates shared a larger room and had bunks all their own. Many ships reserved another cabin for boatsteerers and tradesmen. Of course, the captains had the best rooms available. Some had an actual suite—two rooms with a double bed, a small couch, a desk with a chair, even a wardrobe. The captain's stateroom aboard the *Gypsy* was especially fine. "All his furniture in style and finish would have done credit to a well-appointed drawing room," wrote one observer.

All whalers were allowed a small sea chest for personal belongings. Sea chests contained blankets, clothes, and personal items, such as letters, portraits, razors, combs, and perhaps small musical instruments. Whalers could tell a lot about a sailor from the contents of his sea chest. "From the class of books which his trunk contained," wrote Nathaniel Taylor about a man on the *Julius Caesar*, "I had no hesitation in pronouncing him a scholar."

LIFE BELOW DECK

Sailors tried to spend as little time in the sleeping quarters as possible. Not only were the bunk rooms cramped, they were usually wet. During high winds, waves broke over the decks and seawater made its way below. Rainstorms soaked sailors to the bone. Staying dry was an accomplishment. "I had hoped to have been able to have slept in dry clothes this watch," mourned John Perkins aboard the *Tiger*, "not having done it for several days." Being dry was not just a comfort but also a matter of health. "All the boatsteerers, carpenters, [and] coopers sick with colds, owing to wet berths to sleep in," wrote Nathaniel Morgan aboard the *Hannibal*.

Sailors spent most of their time outside, so weather played a big part in everyday life. In the tropics, whalers baked in the heat and the sun. In the polar regions, temperatures often dropped below zero. Sometimes ice formed, locking the ship in place for days. "Not a spot of water big enough to float the Ship in," read a journal from an Arctic voyage. "The looks are enough to freeze one, to see nothing but ice around." Ice jams were potentially disastrous. Solid ice pushed against ships with enormous pressure that often snapped ships into pieces.

Storms at sea could also be life threatening. "The wind fairly howled and screamed through the rigging like someone in agony," wrote a sailor about a particularly brutal gale. During storms, sailors worked themselves into exhaustion taking down the sail, keeping the ship more or less upright, and making sure the mast did not crack in two. The man at the wheel had to hang on with all his strength. If he lost his grip, the ship would careen out of control. Everything

Many factors made a whaler's voyage difficult, but stormy weather was life threatening.

loose had to be tied down. The stakes were high. The *Desdemona* lost two whaleboats in a storm. The *Delia Hodgkins* was destroyed in another, and five crewmen were killed.

HARDTACK AND SALT JUNK
Most ships left home carrying plenty of food for the voyage, to be replenished in other ports as needed, but the food had almost no variety. The main staple was a hard bread sometimes called hardtack. Made from flour and water, it was nutritious enough, if not very tasty. For protein, crewmen usually were given "salt horse" or "salt junk"—meat or fish preserved in barrels of salt. It didn't take long for sailors to grow weary of the unvarying diet. "The poor fellows fore the mast [the common sailors who bunked in the forecastle] get

nothing but salt junk and hardtack," wrote Will Woods. He may have been exaggerating, but not by much.

Ships did stock other foods, including coffee, sugar, molasses, and sometimes potatoes or onions. The *Nathaniel P. Tallmadge* left home in 1854 carrying four barrels of pickles, eight of vinegar, and five of dried cornmeal. Still, that was not much compared to the thousands of pounds of hardtack and salted meat the ship also packed. And like the hardtack and meat, any food brought along in bulk grew drab before long. "We have a taste of beans six times in the week," complained John States aboard the *Nantasket*.

To complicate matters, many ships had trouble finding good cooks. "He can't cook nor do nothing else," said one captain about the man he had hired. Sometimes sailors were not aware of the problem until after the ship had sailed. "The new cook took upon himself the duties of his office for the first time," mourned John Perkins of the *Tiger*, "and proved himself wholly incompetent."

Without refrigeration, food easily went bad. Often the steward would open a cask of flour, bread, or salt pork to find that the contents were rancid or full of bugs. The food was usually fed to the sailors anyway. William Abbe described his dinner as "literally filled with dirt and cockroaches. I didn't eat a morsel." Will Woods knew the feeling. The hardtack, he charged, was so full of maggots that he had seen it "crawl two feet away from the fellows that were eating it."

Some captains and owners stinted on the food they made available to sailors. On one voyage of the *George*, for instance, the owner instructed the captain to keep the men on short rations, except when they actually caught whales. "A bucket full of boiled coffee without molasses," wrote John States, describing a typical breakfast aboard his ship, "a scanty supply of salt beef with hard, wormy bread constitutes [the] meal and of this, bad as it is, they have not enough."

Greedy captains and owners also created other food-related problems. The captain of the *Hero* once refused to buy extra wood at an island in the Pacific Ocean. He thought the asking price was too high, so he ordered the crew to sail to the Arctic without enough wood to cook more than one meal a day. "It is now 40 days since we were deprived of warm breakfasts and suppers," mourned one of the *Hero*'s crew. "What profiteth a man if he gain the whole world but in the meantime starveth to death?"

DISCIPLINE AND PUNISHMENT

The captain and the mates meted out punishment for any infraction of the rules. There were many rules. Sailors who fell asleep on duty could expect punishment. The captain also punished those he believed to be giving less than their best effort. On some ships, the list of crimes seemed endless: no wearing shoes while making sails, no swearing, no leaving the ship in port. Each offense was punishable, and few captains went easy on their crews.

By modern standards, many of the punishments seem cruel indeed. Men who broke rules could have tar slathered over their faces or sticks shoved up their nostrils. Some sailors were handcuffed. Others were "seized"—tied in the rigging so that their feet barely brushed the ground. Flogging, or whipping, was almost universal. On the *Tiger*, a man who was suspected of stealing was seized and given two dozen strokes with the whip. A few strokes sufficed to tear open the flesh on a sailor's back. But at the time, penalties like this were routine and even considered mild. On the *Julius Caesar*, two men who had fought were seized for half an hour. Nathaniel Taylor wrote afterward that many crew members were surprised by the "leniency" of the punishment.

Punishments were even worse if a captain was unusually mean. W. H. Reynard of the *Canada* beat one or another crew member nearly every day, often with scant justification. "For a frivolous offence," a crewman wrote angrily, Reynard "seized the Steward up in the Mizzen rigging and gave him 1 Doz[en] Clouts." Some days later, Reynard flogged the steward sixty strokes, then shut the man up in the ship's hold for six weeks.

The captain of the *Condor* beat Daniel Hall for pretending to box with a friend. Captain Sluman Gray of the *Hannibal* came close to killing a few crewmen. "Between 4 and 6 pm the Capt[ain] kicked and pounded John Bull (a Kanacker) at the wheel so that he can scarcely move," wrote an appalled Nathaniel Morgan. "This is not the first man he has pounded." Captain William Worth of the *Rambler* flogged a crewman who had taken some extra food. The flogging, wrote a sailor who saw the beating, "left scars he will carry to his

Harsh discipline, such as flogging, was carried out publicly on board whaling ships.

grave. And this was all for taking a small fish and dividing among us, where we were hungry."

MUTINY AND DESERTION

With treatment like this, perhaps it was no wonder that sailors occasionally mutinied. Far from home, seasick, cramped, and poorly fed, men who were routinely beaten and overworked sometimes felt that they had no recourse except rebellion. Although captains were able to stop most mutinies and punish the leaders, a few rebellions were successful. Cyrus Plummer shot his captain aboard the *Junior,* then commandeered the whaleboats and escaped. Isaac Hussey captained two ships whose crews mutinied. On the *Planter,* he killed the crewman who was the ringleader. Five years later, he captained the *William Penn.* This time a different set of mutineers killed him.

Crewmen who were fed up with their treatment also sometimes deserted, or left the ship without permission. Some were fleeing from abusive captains. "We were free!" Daniel Hall exulted after he and a friend slipped away into the Siberian wilderness. "Free from a life of slavery—free from tyranny." Others simply hated whaling. "I just begin to find out that whaling will never do for me," wrote W. R. Bailey aboard the *Caroline* when it docked in San Francisco Bay, "and have determined to leave my ship here if possible." He did, and he never returned to it.

But even sailors who did not really mind their whaling experiences sometimes chose to desert. Whaling ships stopped for supplies at ports and islands across the globe, and the allure of these exotic places was great. Polynesia, in particular, drew thousands of men away from their ships. The hope of a lazy life, with fruit, warm weather, beaches, blue skies, and nearly naked women appealed to many sailors. "On shore we find many people of mixed races," wrote Erastus Bills about the South Pacific. "Englishmen, Yankees, Kanakas, and runaway sailors living with Kanaka women. . . . Everyone seems to be taking life easy." According to one estimate, nearly one-third of all sailors deserted at some point—often in the Pacific islands.

Few of these "beachcombers" stayed permanently, however. Not all the locals were willing to help or even accept the newcomers. Some made staying especially hard. The royal family of Tahiti helped themselves to the property of many deserters, for instance. Other deserters grew to dislike life on the islands. Bugs and other pests were everywhere. "One can throw a saddle on the cockroaches," a deserter wrote in disgust. "The scorpions, centipedes, and spiders are either dangerous or revolting." Many of the beaches turned out to be hard and rocky, and the lagoons were full of barbed fish that made poor eating. Deserters longed for friends and relatives at home, too. The deserter who had hoped to stay in the South Seas forever typically signed aboard another passing whaling ship and wound up back in New England.

BURIAL AT SEA

Poor nutrition, backbreaking physical labor, and excessive heat and cold brought on many illnesses. Once a few men were stricken, the cramped quarters and the damp conditions aboard ship helped spread the diseases. At times whole crews were laid up with one illness or another. "Those that were well had to attend to the sick," wrote Nelson Haley about an outbreak aboard the *Charles W. Morgan*. "The ship for a time was more like a hospital than anything else."

A handful of ships carried men with medical training, but a ship's "doctor" was usually its captain. Most knew very little about healing. Some made sick sailors worse with ineffective pills and outdated remedies. Captain John Simmons of the *Cleone* consulted a medical book to find out what was wrong when he took ill. The answer shocked him. "As near as he could understand it," reported a crewman, "he had got but a few days longer to live." Simmons prepared to die, even promoting the fourth mate to captain. But Simmons's assessment was wrong. He fully recovered.

Certain diseases were more prevalent than others. The dirty and bloody work, the sharing of bunks, and the poor air circulation below decks all contributed to tuberculosis, influenza, and the common cold. Contaminated water led to stomach disorders like diarrhea and dysentery. Poor diet could cause scurvy, a potentially fatal illness characterized by muscle weakness, unexplained bleeding, and loss of teeth. Probably the most feared disease was smallpox, which was contagious and usually led to death. "The small pox has got in the fleet and is raging pretty bad on board some of the Ships," wrote William Ashley aboard the *Governor Troup.* "There has been quite a number died of it."

Death aboard ship from accident and disease was common enough. Yet it was always a sad and sobering experience for those who remained. Because crewmen lived and worked so closely together, the loss of any sailor was keenly felt. "His decease has caused a gap which will never be filled," wrote a sailor aboard the *Tiger* after a foremast hand died. The dead man, the writer continued, was "beloved by all & bound to us by ties which none can appreciate but those who have passed months together within the narrow compass of a ship."

Most dead men were buried at sea. Typically, the crew would gather on the deck near the gangplank, a movable bridge used to board or leave the ship while docked. The sailors would lower the ship's flag and often ring the ship's bell. "The body was wrapped in its coarse winding-sheet [a shroud], laid upon a plank and heavy weights [were] attached," wrote an eyewitness to a funeral. "The men, with uncovered heads, stood in a circle about their comrade, while the captain read the burial service. Then the remains were lifted to the railing and in silence committed to the deep."

A few men, to be sure, were not buried at sea. Some were shipped back to relatives. Sluman Gray of the *Hannibal,* for instance, was placed in a barrel of whiskey to preserve him and sent to New England. A Connecticut man returned home in a cask filled with brine. If a man died near a port, crew members might bury the body on land. From the Aleutians near the Arctic to the island of Saint Paul in the Indian Ocean, whalers erected tombstones with inscriptions like this one: "Sacred to the Memory of Pardon Howland who fell from the mast head of the ship *Midas* of New Bedford and was killed, aged 13 years, 1842."

WHISTLE WHILE WE WORK

It was hard to find time for play, but crews did relax on board ship and have fun. Once life had settled into a routine, scenes such as this one, reported by a crew member of the *Lucy Ann*, became more common:

> Some [of the men] were half naked sitting in their bunks smoking pipes, some eating fat pork, bean soup and other delicacies. One was eating cheese out of an old hat, the Cook in the corner mending his shirt, the steward dancing . . . and I writing Log, and the tobacco smoke as thick as a London fog.

When days were fair and there were no whales, crewmen got out dominoes, checkerboards, or decks of cards and spent lazy afternoons playing games. On several ships, crewmen liked to play hunt the slipper, a game in which one man hid an object for others to find. Some crewmen took their games very seriously. On the *Kathleen*, a harpooner noted, "all hands, except the man at the wheel and those on lookout, stood around watching every move [of a checkers match], even the captain."

Crew members had other pastimes, too. Literate men read whatever was on hand—books, newspapers, letters from home. Many sailors had animal mascots: parrots, cats, dogs, even monkeys. Occasionally these mascots provided not just entertainment but also excitement. "Shag the dog fell overboard this afternoon," wrote the teenage son of the *Rosa Baker*'s captain. "Lowered a boat and got him. . . . He was in the water about 5 min."

And crew members often did crafts. Scrimshaw was especially popular. Invented on whaling ships, scrimshaw was the art of carving designs into whalebone. Typically, sailors etched the designs onto the bone with a needle, then filled in the lines with ink, soot, or tobacco juice. Sailors also made wooden ship models, coconut shell water dippers, and jewelry from tortoiseshell and shark teeth.

Most crew members used some of their time off to catch up on personal chores, such as cutting hair, mending clothes, or bathing. "This morning," wrote Robert Weir, "I am engaged in making a bed quilt of calico and strips of blanket—in preparation for cold & comfortless times that we expect off the Cape [of Good Hope]." Sailors became especially good at sewing. "It is a most surprising thing to

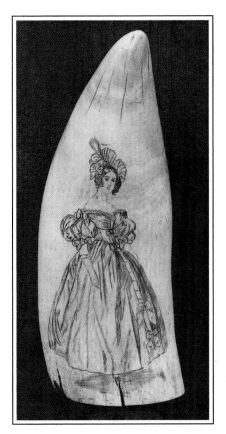 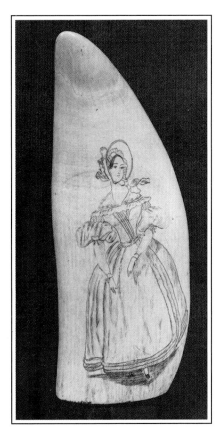

Sailors etched intricate designs, called scrimshaw, into whalebone or, like these, sperm whale teeth.

Chores, music, and crafts were popular pastimes on board whaling ships as was gamming, or talking, to other crew members.

see a before-the-mast man, with great, hairy tarry hands, doing the finest kind of needle work," commented an observer. "So fine, accurate, and tasteful, often in colors, as to be a wonder."

Music was a particularly good way to pass the time. Songs were not only sung for fun, but they also helped make the endless work seem more tolerable. Moreover, when sailors were doing work that required keeping a steady rhythm, such as hoisting the anchor, music helped keep the beat. Some whaling songs complained about life aboard a whaling ship. Others were collections of random verses, often obscene, sung by one crew member while the rest responded with a chorus. Still other songs commented on current events, told stories of real ships and crewmen, or spoke of the future with hope.

Many crewmen were enthusiastic musicians. Some brought along instruments of their own, and others made them. "A jack [sailor] had begged an old flour sieve from the steward," reported Nathaniel Taylor aboard the *Julius Caesar*, "over which he fastened the dried stomach of a blackfish, and with some bits of tin and copper to make a jangle he had constructed a bona fide tambourine." Aboard the *Illinois*, Elias Trotter bragged, "We have in the forecastle 4 fiddlers, 1 accordion, and [a] flute—nearly all [the] men sing and such a combination of sounds and song, men seldom hear."

Since voyages could be so monotonous, any change in the daily routine was welcome. Stocking the ships with new supplies and different food brought much needed variety to life on board. When possible, crews supplemented salt junk by catching fish or other wildlife. "We have taken several fine turtles within a few days, weighing from fifty to eighty pounds each," wrote Francis Olmstead on the *North America*, "which made a very pleasant interlude in our accustomed fare." Another ship anchored near a beach, where the crew got birds, fish, and a bushel of clams. "We shall live high certainly," remarked the captain's wife.

Crews ate best when ships stopped at ports, although this seldom occurred more than once every six months. Journals and letters frequently mentioned the excitement of biting into fresh, unspoiled food. "I don't know that I have ever enjoyed fruit and cheese so much," remarked Robert Weir after his ship stopped in the Azores for supplies. Mary Brewster, a captain's wife who accompanied her husband on the ship, listed some of the food available off the coast of Mexico: "Any quantity of fruit, milk at times as much as we want, fish, Oysters, and fresh beef. Who could not enjoy themselves here?" Of course, too much of even these foods paled after a while. The *Florence* once acquired a huge supply of bananas. "We had them raw or cooked every day for weeks," remembered William Fish Williams, "until I could not smell them without a feeling of nausea."

Food was also important during special occasions. Thanksgiving dinner aboard the *Kathleen* consisted of pork with roasted sweet potatoes, along with a delicacy called "porpoise balls." Other ships, however, downplayed holidays. "Christmas day," noted a crewman on the *Tiger*. "Nothing going on except our usual business." Passing over holidays disturbed some seamen. "Cellebration: Order of the Exercises," Samuel Robertson wrote sarcastically on Independence Day. "Rose in the morning and scrubed of decks."

Sailors created some celebrations that were unique to them. Nearly every ship's crew celebrated making one thousand barrels of oil by frying doughnuts in the try-pots. "Right good they were too," remarked Henrietta Deblois aboard the *Merlin*. "Not the least taste of oil."

The most dramatic and unusual celebration took place when the ship crossed the equator on its way south. A sailor got dressed as Neptune, the Roman god of the sea. Then the veteran sailors put the greenhorn sailors through an initiation ritual. Nathaniel Morgan described his experience:

> The ceremonies were accompanied by various kinds of instrumental music, one instrument being an old piece of an iron hoop drawn across the chine [edge] of an empty water cask. After the questions were finished and satisfactorily answered, I was ordered to be shaved. Accordingly, I was lathered with a *patent chemical* soap, compounded [made] of *Tar* and *Slush* [grease]—and then most delightfully shaved with this *identical* musical iron hoop Eolian [musical] *Razor*. Then, at the word, 'rinse him,' I found myself suddenly ducked backwards into the deck tub full of water.

Morgan got off easily. On other ships, the ritual included shoving tar brushes down the men's throats.

When other whaling ships approached, captains and men often came near enough to share news and gossip. If seas were calm and they had the time, whalers would spend several hours talking, or gamming. Usually, one set of men would row a whaleboat to another ship.

Gamming was a welcome break in the routine. It also provided news of the outside world. "Heard news that the ship *Alex Mansfield* has ben

**As a ship crossed the equator on its way south, new sailors went through
an initiation ritual led by experienced whalers.**

condemnd," one crewman reported rather breathlessly after a gam,
"and Douglass has now got the *France* of [Sag Harbor] and John How-
ell has been kild by a Spurm Whale and the Ship *Pocohontas* foundered
and her Crew was picked up on their way to the Bay of islands." Most
men were glad for the opportunity to see new faces for a change. But a
few men thought there was too much emphasis on gamming. "We
have been chasing some ship around the whole season gamming about
every day," complained a mate aboard the *Lydia*. "Capt. Hathaway had
ought to ship an extra boat's crew for gamming."

FIRST AMERICAN TOURISTS

How soft the breeze through the island trees,
Now the ice is far astern.
Those native maids, those tropical glades
Are awaiting our return . . . .
—"Rolling Down to Old Maui,"
            traditional whaling song

The island of Flores which I passed yesterday was the most beautiful sight I ever saw," wrote Nathaniel Morgan aboard the *Hannibal*. "On a plain are the houses, gardens, fruit trees and plantations of the natives. . . . The whole scenery here is to me new, wild, and beautiful in the extreme."

Flores was in the Azores, 2,500 miles east of New Bedford and a common first stop for a whaling vessel. Like gamming, new food, or crossing the equator, visiting a port helped add spice to a voyage. But Morgan was truly entranced by what he saw. The mountains, flowers, and people of Flores were like nothing he had ever seen in New England.

A few places were not so popular. "This is without exception the most uninviting desolate spot that ever human beings selected for a habitation," wrote one sailor about Paita, Peru. The *Julius Caesar* spent time at an island in the South Atlantic that one crewman called "so savage and repulsive as to make the stoutest heart quail and despair."

In a sense, whalers were the first American tourists. During the nineteenth century, many people never ventured beyond the state in which they were born. The whalers relished the opportunity to explore new cultures and landscapes. They crowded the streets of busy ports in Peru and Angola and wandered down the beaches of the South Sea islands at spots like Tahiti and Tonga. Along the way, these sailors investigated foreign family life, religious ceremonies, art, costume, and language. After visiting some large stone walls on a South Pacific island, Nelson Haley spent many hours wondering who had made them and why. William Fish Williams was fascinated by the canoes of the Solomon Islanders. John States wandered into the middle of a Chilean family funeral, stayed to observe, then wrote about it in his journal. Weston Howland did his own study of Pitcairn Island. "The girls are marriageable at the age of twelve," he claimed, "and mothers of fine children at thirteen. Rather too young for our folks."

"IT IS A BEAUTIFUL ISLAND"

Whaling ships did travel almost everywhere. It would be hard to name a coastline that was not visited by at least one American whaling ship during the nineteenth century. The *Charles W. Morgan* sailed all the way around the world on its voyage of 1849 to 1853. The *Addison* sailed 37,000 miles in one year. Between 1880 and 1884, the *Kathleen* put in at Tristan da Cunha in the South Atlantic Ocean, the Azores in the North Atlantic, the Comoro Islands in the Indian Ocean, and many other mainland ports.

For the sailors, arriving in port was a welcomed vacation from the tedious days at sea. Unfortunately, whaling ships put into port as seldom as possible. Every day in a harbor was a day without whales.

Most captains would dock their ships only for repairs or supplies. For major repairs, recruiting new crewmen, or loading up with enough food to last another five or six months, the captain searched for a big port with plenty of people and stores. For minor repairs, freshwater, or hunting wild animals, however, almost any section of coastline would do.

The larger ports were especially appealing to sailors. Places like Faial (in the Azores), St. Helena (in the South Atlantic), and Oahu (in the Pacific) were full of bars, pawnshops, bowling alleys, and other businesses catering to the whalers. Many sailors used their shore leave to get drunk. "The three public houses drove a rattling trade during the days the men were on shore," remembered Nelson Haley about a New Zealand port, "as they had money to spend and but little chance to spend it for much else than drink." Fights were common, especially after lots of liquor. "We have now had altogether eight days of liberty," wrote a cabin boy aboard the *Ahab* in Talcahuano, Chile. "The necessary and indispensable amount of broken heads, black eyes, bloody noses and otherwise damaged countenances [faces] has been given and received."

MEETING THE ISLANDERS

Once in a while, sailors would land at a completely deserted island, but ships more often made stops in places where at least a few people lived. Sailors usually judged the people they saw by the standards of home. They were at once fascinated and also disapproving, although some were more tolerant of what they saw than others.

A few whalers took a strong disliking to the people they met. Some gave no specific reason. "Our deck has been covered day & night by Spaniards," wrote a man as his ship left Callao in Peru. "A Spaniard I do not like." Others accused those they met of laziness and immorality. The scant clothing worn by many tropical peoples appalled some straitlaced New Englanders. Hawaiians were "a low, degraded, indolent set," reported one observer. "Both sexes bathe in the water entirely naked, unabashed." The Maori of New Zealand, on the other hand, were considered violent and brutal. A crewman aboard the *Julian* called them "treacherous," while a sailor on the *Nimrod* described them as a "barbarous race."

The Maoris were not the most dangerous people a whaler might meet, however. According to popular legends of the time, the world was full of cannibals—people who ate human flesh. The *Beaver* had a boatsteerer who complained of poor treatment. "He was put ashore by Captain Rogers on a cannibal island," a newspaper reported, "where he was eaten." Most whalers were willing to accept the story as true. "It is said [the Christmas Islands] are inhabited by cannibals," wrote Mary Brewster as her ship sailed nearby. "I feel anxious till we

The New Zealand Maori were among the many peoples visited by nineteenth-century whalers.

get clear of them." Weston Howland stated as fact that most people from Nuku Hiva, an island in the South Pacific, were "very savage, and cannibals."

While it is unlikely that any crewman ever was eaten, not all locals were friendly. The *Osceola* was attacked by Malay tribesmen. The crew fought back with boiling water and harpoons, and, in one gory detail, the cooper chopped off the hands of several men who tried to board the ship. Newspapers often reported disasters with headlines such as "Massacre at the Fegee [Fiji] Islands."

Still, most whalers liked, and sometimes even admired, the people they saw. Some gave them faint praise. "Though not civilized," wrote John States about the natives of a South Pacific island, "[they] are not by any means to be ranked with savages." Others were much more positive. "Never have I met with any people who pleased me so much as the Kanakers," wrote a crewman aboard the *Tiger*. William Allen thought the Tahitians were wonderful. "I never heard such beautiful singers," he wrote. "Their voices are finer than ever I heard in any other place."

IRON FOR BANANAS

In most parts of the world, whalers traded with the local people. Ships frequently carried cloth, metal, liquor, or gunpowder to trade for fresh food. The *Hope* gave a group of islanders tobacco in exchange for chickens and eggs. Individual crewmen did the same. "I traded about a dozen small needles, a jacket, twenty skeins of thread, and some pieces of iron," reported John States, "receiving in return twelve large bunches of bananas [and] one hundred fine apples" and several other items. Other ships and seamen received wood, pigs, pieces of art, sweet potatoes, beef, and furs for the trade goods they had brought along.

Many crewmen believed they were taking advantage of the locals. Some laughed at the natives' gullibility. The crew of the *Ceres* got coconuts and fruit in trade for what one sailor dismissed as "small pieces of iron hoop, spikes, old tin, beads or any old thing that is of no value." The *Hannibal* picked up two boatloads of fruit for a bag of bread and a few pounds of tobacco. Most whalers didn't seem to feel guilty for cheating the native peoples, but some did note the problems caused by bringing alcohol and tobacco into areas where they were previously unknown. "One ship brought out 60 barrels [of rum]," George Pritchard wrote about Tahiti, "another 40 and many others large quantities. This has caused a great deal of intoxication among the natives."

Whether the trades were fair or not is impossible to determine by modern standards. Some historians have blamed whalers for helping to destroy traditional cultures, especially in Polynesia. Not only did the locals give up their wood, meat, and fruit in these trades, but they gained nothing of lasting value. They got clothes, which were not really necessary in warm climates, and a few iron nails that did not improve construction very much. The introduction of tobacco, alcohol, and firearms all had dreadful effects.

Other historians, however, believe that the locals got what they wanted in these trades. It is true that islanders traded of their own free will. Whaling captains rarely used force, or the threat of force, against local people. There were a few abuses, to be sure. Some captains threatened to destroy villages if the locals did not give them what they wanted. But using force made little sense. Whalers needed sources of food and water. Angering the local populations would have jeopardized future trade.

AT HOME, AT SEA

Adieu to my comrades, for a while
we must part.
And likewise the lass who has fair
won my heart. . . .
　　　—"Farewell to Tarwathie,"
　　　　traditional whaling song

I feel very lonely tonight," wrote Hannah Blackmer to her husband, Seth, a whaling captain, in 1864. "I have been alone with the children all day, and the little ones are all asleep, and it is very quiet indeed. Seth, can I ever wait a *whole year* (perhaps more) before I can see you?"

Very few jobs separated families as much as whaling did. Farmers spent the day in the fields, but they came home at night. Storekeepers lived near their shops. Even sailors on clipper ships followed a schedule that brought them home every few weeks. But when whalers sailed, they left friends, parents, wives, and children behind for years at a time. "In fifteen years of whaling life, I have spent just seventeen months at home," lamented one sailor. During such long voyages, both those at home and those at sea were lonely. Hannah Blackmer's letter could have been written by any number of women across New England. Many whaling men felt the same.

"MR. PAUL C. BURGESS, SHIP *CHELSEA*, PACIFIC OCEAN"

At best, communication in nineteenth-century America was an adventure. Without telephones, radios, or computers, letters were the most reliable way of getting in touch with others. Typically, letters were written on one side of a sheet of paper and then folded so that the writing faced in. The blank side served as the envelope. Stamped, sealed, and addressed, the letter was ready to go. But without good transportation, mail could take days or weeks to get to its destination. Letters written home by whalers were famous for arriving weeks late.

Delivery to whaling ships was even harder. A letter to a whaler could not be addressed much beyond the name of the sailor and the ship on which he sailed. Whalers spent most of their time in the middle of the ocean, miles from land, let alone a post office. Worse, the ships moved constantly. Most people on land followed the example of Ann Burgess, the wife of Captain Paul Burgess of the *Chelsea*. Ann addressed her letters to Mr. Paul C. Burgess, Ship *Chelsea*, Pacific Ocean, and sent them aboard ships sailing from New Bedford. Those ships would carry the letters toward the Pacific.

But the odds of the mail ever reaching Paul were poor. If a captain happened upon the *Chelsea* at sea or in a harbor, Paul would get his letter. If the ships did not meet, the captain might pass the letters on to other ships or entrust mail to a storekeeper at a popular port. Still, most letters never reached the intended recipient. As a result, Ann sent important information several different times. "I have written a whole sheet over," she wrote, "which I shall send by one of the ships and this by another and so try to write the news in all." When their son was born, the Burgesses got lucky. Paul received one of the six letters that Ann sent, and it arrived only six months after the baby's birth.

"KNOW LETTERS FOR POOR ME"

At either end, receiving a letter was cause for excitement. "Yours [your letter] of Jan. 5th I received by the *William Gifford*," wrote Charles Pierce to his wife Eliza in 1862. "You had better believe I was glad." William Almy and his wife, Almira, on board the *Cape Horn Pigeon*, once picked up seventeen letters at a Peruvian port. "What a feast now, a pleasure we have never known before," Almira wrote. "We were almost beside ourselves with joy." Hannah Blackmer, back home in New Bedford, was equally delighted to get mail. "I am so happy tonight, dear Seth, for I have had three letters from you this week," she wrote to him in 1864.

Letters that did arrive were treasured. "Read my letters over again for the 7000th time," wrote Benjamin Boodry of the *Arnolda*. "Have got the whole 25 of them by hart." Sailors who rarely got mail sometimes bought letters from other men, even though they did not know the people who had sent them. Even whalers who could not read or write nevertheless saw the importance of mail. An illiterate crewman aboard the *Kathleen* asked Bob Ferguson to take dictation so he could send his girlfriend a letter. "It was *some* letter," Ferguson remembered years later.

Letters provided such a link to the outside world that getting no mail seemed disastrous. "I hav not got eny letters," wrote John Deblois to his wife Henrietta. "Oh what a disapointment it is to me." Charlotte Dehart, who accompanied her husband, captain of the *Roman 2,* wrote, "Know letters for poor me." Relatives at home felt the same way. "We have had no word of our Son Sence he Sailed from your Port," wrote an anxious set of parents to a ship's agent. "The time Appears very Long." As time went on without any mail, many men and women began to fear the worst. "My Wife, my children and friends, where are they?" wondered Daniel Baldwin aboard

Letters and news from a whaling ship were precious to those left at home.

the *Charleston.* "Are they in life or are they dead? I have not had news from them for the long space of 2½ years."

NEWS!

As time went on, whaling families found ways of making communication a little easier. Some ships' officers wrote to their local newspapers. "A letter has been received at the office from one of the mates of the *Vermont,*" read an item in an 1836 issue of the Poughkeepsie, New York, *Telegraph.* "The crew were all well and perfect harmony prevailed." The *Vermont* was a local ship, with many crew members from the Poughkeepsie area. The *Telegraph*'s good news reached more people than individual letters could have.

The most important newspaper for whaling families, however, was the *Whalemen's Shipping List* of New Bedford. Written for whalers, shipowners, and those at home, the *Whalemen's Shipping List* gave weekly updates on every American whaling ship. Along with other data, the editors noted where the ship was most recently sighted, the month and year it had sailed, and the port it hailed from. Sometimes the news was recent. More often, however, information was months out of date. Week after week went by, and the listing for the ship never changed. It was frustrating for friends, relatives, and for those at sea. "I see by the *Shipping List*," remarked Lucy Gifford in a letter from Chile, "we are not reported since leaving Fayal" in the Azores, thousands of miles away.

The *Whalemen's Shipping List* also published ads of interest to mariners, along with information about oil prices, news of ship sales, and notices of disasters at sea. The disasters made receiving the *Shipping List* a nerve-wracking experience for many at home. "The ship *Wm. Hamilton . . .* was lost on the 27th of January last," began a news item in 1856. Luckily for relatives of the men on the ship, the article concluded with the comforting words, "The officers and crew are all safe." Not all families were so fortunate. An 1871 story reported that Lemuel Eldridge of the *Laconia* "fell from the main top the day before, and was instantly killed. His age was 18."

HOMESICKNESS

Homesickness began early for many whalemen. What seemed like a grand adventure before sailing soon became a long, boring, dangerous stretch of years without wives, mothers, children, or friends. "My feelings on leaving my home and friends cannot be described," a teenager wrote gloomily a few days out. Nathaniel Taylor was close to thirty when the *Julius Caesar* left New London in 1851, but he did not have an easier time leaving his family. "Sadly I had felt," he remembered, "as my feeble but fond mother embraced me and murmured a faint 'Good-bye, my son.'"

The diaries of men at sea spoke often of their loneliness and their desire to see friends and family again. "Home Sick, Sea Sick, Love Sick, Heart Sick," wrote a sailor aboard the *Clifford Wayne*. "I am getting real lonesome lately," another man wrote to his wife, "and I begin to feel as though it would help me if I could see you for a few minutes."

Worse, whalers knew when they sailed that they might never see some of their loved ones again. In the three or four years that a whaling ship would be gone, things would change. Friends might leave town, children would grow older, relatives could die. Seldom did the most recent letter carry news that was completely current. Charles Pierce took no chances: He sent mail to his wife with the greeting "My Dear Wife if Living." The *California* was almost home when it chanced to gam another ship just leaving the harbor. The ship brought the *California*'s captain the sad news that his wife had just died. Scenes like this were all too common.

BACK HOME

In some ways, separation was even harder on families at home. While husbands and fathers were exploring the oceans in whaling ships, wives and children were going on with ordinary existence—alone. For those onshore, reminders of the menfolk were everywhere. "Today I put your suit of clothes and overcoat on [the] line to air," wrote Phoebe Sherman. Clothing, knickknacks, books—almost anything could spark memories of days when men had been home.

Wives who stayed onshore were often called widows, because their husbands were gone so long, they might almost have been considered dead. Men who made several voyages were away from their wives for impossibly long periods. "We have been married five years and lived together ten months, It is too bad, too bad," wrote Harriet Gifford. "O my dear, I cannot [imagine] you are gone to stay[.] It seems all the time as if you were coming back soon," mourned Ann Burgess. "My Dear Husband what shall I say, I don't want to write I want to talk with you." In 1827 Mary T. Smith poured out her frustrations in a letter to her husband Parker aboard the *Connecticut*:

> I am a social being capable of enjoying the society of my friends and am often happy in their company. . . . But this, my dear Parker, does not make up the loss I sustain in being deprived of your agreeable company and when I consider the distance we are apart and the length of time we must be separated and the innumerable trials and dangers to which we are exposed, my heart faints within me and I am ready to exclaim, "Why is it thus?"

Some women found ingenious ways of making the voyages seem shorter. "Last night I shortened the four years by calculation," Phoebe Sherman explained to her husband. "2 years, 8 months only for active life if in bed by 10 and up at 6. When asleep I shall not realize your absence."

Children, however, could not rationalize the loss of their fathers so

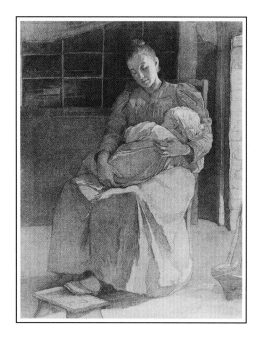

Many whalers' children grew up virtually fatherless.

easily. "The children express a great anxiety to see you," one mother wrote. Some children were too young to understand how far away their fathers were and how long it would take them to return home. For others, the time and distances were all too clear. "Papa will never see me a little girl again, will he?" Hannah Blackmer's daughter Jennie asked.

It was true. Whalers missed huge pieces of their children's lives. Paul Burgess met his son for the first time when the boy was two years, four months old. This was a common scenario. "I did not feel very well acquainted with him," one New Bedford girl said about her father years later. "He stood out as a wonderful being who was with us occasionally for a brief period."

DOING THE WORK OF TWO

For the women and children left behind, the nights were lonely, but the days were filled with chores. Most women spent their time cooking, cleaning, and caring for the children. Yet the bills still had to be paid, the house kept up, and the crops planted. These responsibilities came to rest on the wives.

In most northeastern communities, it was difficult for a woman to live on her own. Nineteenth-century New England was a man's world. Men made the decisions at home and had authority over wives and children. Women's roles were severely limited. Few women held jobs outside the home.

So it was hard for many wives to take over the running of the household. Some worried that their husbands would find fault with their decision making. Others felt overwhelmed by the work. "I spend so much money I get discouraged," wrote one woman. "I try to spend only what is necessary, but you will forgive me if I spend more than I ought, for I do not know how now, but I think I will learn." A few women, though, delighted in their freedom to do more than the average New England wife. "I have let [rented] my house to a Mr. Austin Harris from the harbor's mouth," Mary T. Smith informed her husband. It was her decision, not his. That decision would have been rare in a non-whaling community.

For most families onshore, money was an issue. Whalers often supported wives, children, or parents, but they were not paid on a regular basis. As a result, families scrambled for whatever they could get. Some wives, especially those whose husbands had already sailed once or more, relied on savings. Others had the help of family and friends. Still others earned money by selling vegetables or by hiring themselves out to clean other people's homes.

It was also possible for some women to get advances on their husbands' pay. Shipowners made arrangements for such advances, but their willingness to help out families in need varied. Hannah Ashley, whose husband, William, was first mate on the *Governor Troup*, received thirty dollars every other month from the owners of the ship. Others had to make formal requests each time there was a need. "If you Could let me have 15 or 20 dollar," wrote Sophia Brown to the owners of her son's ship, "it would enable [me] to git a Long till i am better able to work agane." The whalers themselves approved of these payments, although the money advanced had to be repaid with interest from their eventual earnings. "I alwais intend that my mother shall enjoy all the comforts of life," wrote Leonard Gifford to the owners of the *Hope*. "Advance her any reasonable amount."

THE MOTHER SHIP

Families left at home did have one advantage: Every whaling "widow" in New Bedford, New London, or Hudson knew others in the same situation. Whaling ports were full of wives without husbands, elderly parents without sons, and children without fathers. The absence of men and the emphasis on seafaring made whaling ports very different from other cities and towns. With many of the men away, women had more responsibilities at home. Early women's rights advocate Lucretia Mott, who was born on Nantucket in 1793, attributed her feminism in part to living in a whaling town. As an adult, Mott lived in several larger cities in the Northeast and was shocked to discover that none of these cities allowed women such an obvious presence in community business.

One historian has described the island of Nantucket during whaling days as the Mother Ship, or home base, for the ships. The same could be said for any whaling port. Ports had a huge economic stake in whaling. The New Bedford city directory of 1856 listed nineteen different oil- and candle-producing factories. One year, sixty-five whaling ships sailed out of New Bedford, carrying a total of 32,500 barrels of freshwater, one thousand tons of iron hoops, and much more. These much needed supplies were provided by local coopers, carpenters, blacksmiths, and merchants. Newspapers carried ads for maritime insurance companies, nautical instrument makers, bakers who specialized in bread for ship use, and druggists who offered "Ships' Medicine Chests furnished at short notice."

And, in every whaling community, ties to the ships went far beyond moneymaking. When a ship came into port, nearly everyone in town had an interest in seeing who was on board. Families never knew for sure when a ship would arrive. Wives and parents had to be constantly on the alert and tried not to be too disappointed if a ship was weeks or months late. But when a ship did arrive, a crowd was usually there to meet it. Even people who did not have family members on board rushed down to the docks. The ship might carry letters or news of other ships. In Hudson, New York, a preacher began Sunday worship with the words: "I am so glad to see so many at service, even though the *American Hero* has arrived." The arrival of the ship was news to everyone present, and in a few moments the church was empty. The entire congregation left for the docks.

The arrival of a particular ship did not necessarily mean that all the crewmen who had left on the ship had come home. A wife could not be sure that her husband had returned until he actually walked off the ship. Some sailors had deserted in midvoyage. Others had died. Families may not have heard the news before the ship returned.

The departure and arrival of whaling ships always drew a crowd.

With communication as unreliable as it was, some family members never did find out exactly what had happened to their missing son, husband, or brother. A young sailor aboard the *Kathleen* died on the ship and was buried at sea. "We wondered how this poor boy's mother would feel when she gets the news a year from now or maybe longer," Robert Ferguson wrote. "It is hard to tell if she will hear at all."

People went to the docks to see the ships off, too. "Notwithstanding the inclemency of the weather, we think nearly 2000 persons were present," reported a newspaper when the *Nathaniel P. Tallmadge* set sail for the first time in 1836. "She was decorated with flags and enlivened by excellent music from the Poughkeepsie Band." The ships were part of the community, and the community's fate was linked to the ships.

FAMILIES ON BOARD

Oh who'd not be a sailor's wife
And brave the Ocean's waves
And sail with him o'er seas of foam
Above the coral caves. . . .
  —Mrs. William Swain, aboard
      the ship *Clifford Wayne*

I sometimes think if you go round Cape Horn again I shall go with you for I cannot be left so long if it possible to avoid it. Yours in greatest love, Ann Burgess."

Ann Burgess's letter to her husband, Paul, spoke for many women who could not bear the loneliness of separation. So far as we know, Ann never did go whaling with her husband. Other women, however, did join their husbands aboard their ships. According to some estimates, by the 1860s about one of every five captains was bringing his wife along. Many of the women who chose to sail were childless. But a few mothers did bring their children.

Most of these women sailed for only one reason: Whatever the cost, they wanted to be with their husbands. "Samuel is all the world to me," Mary Chipman Lawrence told her brother when he questioned her decision to join her husband at sea. "Why should we live with half the globe between us?" Other women felt the same way.

"Poor mortals, to never know when we are well off," sighed Lucy Ann Crapo, "but I wanted to come so as to have a home, and I am not sorry." While a few women went to sea in search of adventure or to improve their health—the fresh salt air was thought to be healing—most women who sailed cited their love for their husbands as their reason.

Captains seemed happy to have their wives along. Leonard Brownson of the *Baltic* expected to meet his wife in Honolulu and bring her aboard for a whaling cruise. As the ship approached Hawaii, a crewman wrote that Brownson "is looking as smiling as a basket of Chips." Indeed, having a wife along was often the husband's idea. John Deblois was crushed when his wife, Henrietta, refused to join him aboard the *Merlin*. "You may ask what shall be don[e] with the house and things at home," he wrote to her in 1861. "All I can say is to do just what you mind to do with them[. It] will please me if you will only *come to me*." She never did.

"A WOMAN'S PLACE IS IN THE HOME"

Many of the women who did sail faced difficulties. The notion that women belonged at home was widespread during the nineteenth century. New England society frowned on wives who attempted to break from their traditional roles. Families and friends tried to talk many whaling wives out of going. Mary Brewster's mother was furious. "[She] said her consent would never be given[,] in no way would she assist me and if I left her she thought me very ungrateful," Brewster reported on the first page of her diary. Her decision to go meant that she was no longer welcome in her mother's house. Mary Ann Sherman's family reacted even more harshly. When she chose to sail with her husband, her parents declared her dead and set up a tombstone in the local cemetery to prove it.

Many crew members were also against having women on board. There was an old belief, which lasted into the 1840s, that women jinxed a whaler. Crewmen often feared that wives would try to stop the swearing, drinking, and womanizing in which many indulged. Some crewmen found the wives stuck-up and unfriendly. "She never speaks to any of the other officers when on deck but her husband," John Perkins wrote of Mary Brewster. Perhaps more important, women took up space aboard the already cramped ship.

Most shipowners didn't approve of women aboard whaling ships either. Owners expected a captain to take certain risks, including lowering the boats in bad weather, leading the chase himself, and maneuvering ships through reefs and ice in search of whales. A whaling captain might not choose to take such risks with his wife along. He might therefore come back later or with fewer barrels of oil than would a more aggressive, less safety-conscious captain. Shipowners only grudgingly allowed wives to sail. Some forced conditions on captains. Philip Howland of the *Mary and Susan*, for instance, was told that after two years he could send for his wife—but only if he had collected one thousand barrels of oil by then.

A HONEYMOON SUITE

By shipboard standards, most whaling women lived in luxury. Generally they shared their husbands' quarters. With two living together, space was tight, so some captains carved out extra room. "My Husband has let another Stateroom into ours and now we have a nice large one," wrote Eliza Williams aboard the *Florida*. Other captains built a small shelter on the deck, which wives often used as a retreat. Harriet Swain was delighted when the carpenter aboard her ship began to build one. "I think [it] will be firstrate," she wrote, "it being something I have wanted all the voyage."

Like the men, women brought whatever they could fit on board. Eliza Williams took a kitten to keep her company and a geranium plant for decoration. Elizabeth Stetson found room for one hundred books. A few women managed to fit a keyboard instrument called a melodeon into their quarters. Clothes took up plenty of space, too. Women typically brought heavy cloth dresses, complete with petti-

It was hard for families to lose their daughters to a whaling husband and a life at sea.

coats and all the other trappings of style back at home. Most packed along special reminders of home, too. One woman took a jewel case: "a present from our niece at parting," she wrote a friend, "and not a little valued by us I can assure you."

ADJUSTING TO LIFE AT SEA

It took time for most women to get used to the ship. The rolling sea made it difficult to walk from one end of the stateroom to the other. Eating was almost as hard. "When I seat myself to the table to get my meals," Almira Gibbs complained, "I find most as much in my lap as in my plate and mug." And some women never got used to the storms and the spray from the sea. "Drawers tumbling out," lamented a woman during a gale. "My teapot and pitcher broken."

All of this rocking made most of the women seasick. "Went on board ship at 10:30," wrote Adelaide Wicks. "Was seasick at 3." But unlike the men, who spent most of their time working in the fresh air, the women were restricted to their cabins when nauseated. As a result, they often took weeks to recover. Mary Brewster was too sick to write in her journal for the first month of the *Tiger's* voyage. Experienced sailors suffered as badly as the others. "Seasick," wrote Elizabeth Stetson, who had been to sea many times before. "Eat and then vomit is the order of the day."

WHAT TO DO?

Women who sailed had no official responsibilities aboard ship, but some tasks fell naturally into their hands. Communication was one. The women were expected to help stay in touch with home. Those who published the *Whalemen's Shipping List* actually encouraged women to go on board. The *Shipping List* editors believed that women were more likely than men to send word of position, route, and adventures. They certainly had more time to do so. Women "make capital correspondents," the paper editorialized, "and through the female love of letter-writing, keep us well posted up in the catch and prospects of the season."

Some women also served as surrogate mothers to the youngest crew members—the cabin boys. Scarcely into their teens, many of these boys needed adult attention. "Calls himself 16 years old. [S]hould think he was about 12," wrote Mary Brewster about the *Tiger's* cabin boy. "I am inclined to think he was a bad boy and his Father was glad to ship him of[f]." Mary Stickney gave her ship's cabin boy candy, coconuts, and a shirt at Christmas. Sometimes the cabin boys returned the favors. When the mother of an infant was terribly sick aboard the *South Boston*, the cabin boy took over. "He does everything for the Child," reported an observer approvingly. "He washes and dresses it, feeds it, and puts it to sleep. I don't see what she would do without him."

Women often took on the task of doctoring as well. Most knew little more about medicine than their husbands did, but they tried their best. "I think if I should go to sea again I would take a few lessons in medicine," wrote one wife. Women did what they could to make seriously ill crewmen more comfortable—sometimes they even gave up their accommodations. "I miss my house," mourned Harriet Allen when she gave up her deck retreat so the cook could rest there, "but am glad I have to for Cook's sake."

Only a handful of women ever had any significant role in steering the ship, chasing the whales, or cutting in. Captains rarely consulted their wives about when to put in at port, whether to pursue a whale, or how best to punish men caught fighting. Although the women were pioneers aboard their ships, the men made it clear that they were along for the ride and nothing more.

Many women were frustrated by having so little to do. It was nerve-wracking to watch the whale hunt from shipboard, especially if a husband was one of the men in the whaleboats. "I dread it, much as we want the Oil," wrote Eliza Williams. "I am so fearful that

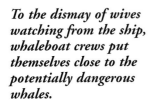
To the dismay of wives watching from the ship, whaleboat crews put themselves close to the potentially dangerous whales.

something will happen, but I will hope for the best." Worse still was watching the boats disappear slowly from sight. Many women felt helpless as their husbands rowed off, perhaps never to return. "This has been a long lonely day for me," wrote Susan McKenzie on the *Hercules*, "as James went away about 4 o'clock AM and did not return till after dark."

During cutting in or when the weather was bad, crewmen sent women below the deck. This step was intended for the women's safety and to give the men more room in which to maneuver. Cutting in was especially difficult for the wives. With the deck covered by whale entrails and the crew working intently on their jobs, women had to stay out of the way. Wives did try to find ways of watching the action. Sallie Smith got into a whaleboat suspended above the deck, and Susan McKenzie perched on the roof of her lean-to, but many women were forced to stay in their cabins.

"I HAVE GOT SO TIRED OF THINKING"

Women struggled to keep busy on board. Sewing and knitting occupied many long hours. Some wives helped mend sails. Others busied themselves making bonnets, napkins, or towels—anything to make life more comfortable. Reading was another common pastime. "If I could not read I don't know what I should do," wrote Almira Gibbs. Several wives joined forces with their husbands to read aloud to each other each day. Mary Brewster had this activity down to a science: "Husband one night and self the next one and so on throughout the week," she wrote.

Many women took time to record their thoughts and daily activities in journals. In these writings, the topic of boredom came up again and again. "I want something new to write about," complained Eliza Williams at one point during the *Florida's* voyage. "I have nothing now but the same thing over and over." After weeks at sea, many women wished for "something new"—anything new. Even a change for the worse was welcome. "I begin to be tired of our fine weather and long for a change," wrote Mary Brewster. "Hardly know what to do to pass the lagging time," wrote another woman. "I have got so tired of thinking," reported yet another. "It is all I have to do to sit and sew and think."

Most women had little interest in the mechanics of the hunt. But a few wives did take a keen interest in whaling and the workings of the ship. Eliza Williams devoted large sections of her diary to descriptions of whales, whaleboats, and the hunt. "It is truly wonderful to me," she wrote, "the whole process, from the taking of the great . . . monster of the deep till the oil is in the casks." Mary Lawrence watched the cutting in aboard the *Addison* with great interest. "I want to see everything that is going on," she wrote. "I may never have another opportunity."

"I FEEL SO LONELY AND HOMESICK"

The boredom was made much worse because nearly every whaling wife was the only woman aboard her ship. While members of the crew had one another for company, the women had only their husbands. Many wives longed for female companionship. "How would you feel to live more than seven months and not see a female face?" wrote Susan Fisher aboard the *Cowper*. "I think I shall hardly know how to speak to a lady," worried Mary Lawrence as her ship approached a port.

Gamming at ports or at sea was a possibility. Unfortunately, many women were not given the chance. In their long skirts and fashionable shoes, women could not easily climb into whaleboats to visit another ship. Sometimes women were raised and lowered into the boats by means of a "gamming chair"—a swinging seat attached to the ship's rail with a rope. However, if the weather were bad or the sea were choppy, many husbands forbade their wives to go—unless, like Cynthia Ellis aboard the *Ohio*, they were able to help row the boats.

Even in fair weather, some husbands did not consider their wives' wishes. Many women were left on board while husbands and other crew members rowed to shore at ports. When Mary Brewster's husband put in at the Juan Fernández Islands, Mary hoped to be invited to visit the island with him. "But I was doomed to be disappointed," she wrote in her journal, "as he thought best for me not to go." The cabin boy did bring her a bunch of flowers, and her husband later regretted not allowing her to come along.

Many men did not realize just how much their wives longed for a break from the tedium of the voyage. "This is the second time he has been aboard to gam where there were ladies I would very much like to see," wrote a despairing Jerusha Hawes aboard the *Emma C. Jones.* "I feel so lonely and homesick but I suppose he does not think—he has never had a wife at sea before—he does not think." It was the last entry in her journal, though the voyage continued many more months.

"HE WAS BORN UPON THE BRIGHT SALT SEA"

A whaling song spoke of a man named Jack, who was "born upon the bright salt sea." The song itself was a tall tale, but the birth of children at sea was not. While unusual, it certainly happened. "Last night we had an addition to our ship's company," wrote a crewman aboard the *Nantasket,* "for at nine PM Mrs Smith was safely delivered of a fine boy whose weight is eight lbs[.] This is quite a rare thing at sea but fortunately no accident happened[.] Had any thing occurred there would have been no remedy and we should have had to deplore the loss of a fine good hearted woman."

Most captains whose wives were pregnant tried to put them ashore before they gave birth, but this was not always feasible. The *Nantasket* had run into foul weather, which delayed it from reaching port. Other ships did manage to drop off women. New England children sometimes had birth certificates marked New Zealand, Hawaii, or St. Helena. With luck, the wives could stay on land for a while after the birth and recover onshore in the company of other women. More often, however, the women—and the new babies as well—quickly re-

Captain James A. M. Earle, like a few other whaling captains, brought his whole family to live on board.

joined the ship. It could be expensive to interrupt a trip, and most shipowners were not very understanding when it came to family problems.

Babies were not the only children on board ship. Several captains left home with their whole families. If the statehouse was barely large enough for two, it was especially tiny when one, two, or even three children were added. Women who sailed with children, of course, had a very different experience from women who sailed without them. With children, there was rarely an idle moment. Children took time and energy. Husbands of the era seldom spent much time with babies to begin with, and whaling captains were far too busy with other work. On land there would have been friends, relatives, and neighbors to offer advice or watch the children for a few hours. But at sea the mother was usually the only one able to take care of them.

Some women resented having to watch the children constantly. The mother of a four year old aboard the *Nautilus* complained that everyone was too "busy to look out for him" when he played on the deck during cutting in. Keeping children properly educated was difficult, too. Lessons were often interrupted by trying out—the process of rendering the blubber into oil. Many times, the ship rolled and pitched too much for kids to concentrate. Many mothers abandoned school after a while but felt guilty about it. "School drags," complained Harriet Allen. "In fact everything drags. The fault is with *me*."

Shipmate Gomes's baby played in a tub cover while on board the whaling ship Wanderer.

On a whaling ship there was nowhere for a growing child to exercise, and there was little room for toys and games. The system of watches on board meant that some crewman was almost always off duty and asleep. Children had to play silently. When the crew of the *Eliza Adams* asked the captain's wife to keep her four children quiet, she refused. Instead, she told the children, as one crewman put it, "to make as much noise as they like, for father owned the ship." Tempers flared, and the problem was never fully resolved.

Having children living on board could also be a lot of fun. Children could brighten the dreariest of voyages. They could also be great companions, especially for the mothers. Mary Lawrence, for example, very much enjoyed having her daughter Minnie aboard the *Addison*. Minnie was five at the beginning of the trip, and her mother proudly recorded many of the child's sayings, questions, and accomplishments along the way.

CHILDREN AT PLAY

Like their mothers and fathers, children varied in their reactions to seafaring. Many children enjoyed the places they visited. "I am in Honolulu," seven-year-old Laura Jernegan, a passenger aboard the *Roman* wrote. "It is a real pretty place." Others were fascinated by the work aboard ship. "He watched every move [the sailors] made," wrote a woman about her seven-year-old son, and "learned the names of all the ropes." Years after her trip on the *Northern Light,* Anna King wrote, "Tried to be as nautical as my father."

Other children liked spending time with the crewmen. "They were my playmates," said Jamie Earle of the crew of the *Charles W. Morgan*, on which he sailed between the ages of three and eight. The ship's second mate made Jamie a toy whaleboat. Even when crew members were too busy to play, they did feel a certain sense of responsibility for the children's well-being. Sailors regularly jumped into the water to rescue children who had gone overboard. Sometimes they risked their lives to rescue pets as well.

But interaction with the crew wasn't always positive. Children saw fights, punishments, and accidents that they would have been better off not seeing. They also missed out on friendships with children their own age. Except for siblings who sailed together, it was unusual for whaling children to see any other children more than once or twice a year. Jamie Earle's parents eventually sent him home for social reasons. "They decided that I'd been away from other children enough," he remembered. Because of the lack of friendships, one observer remarked that whaling children seemed "very young for their ages, both boys and girls."

Shipboard life was also confining for children. Cramped quarters, poor food, and the lack of fresh air in the cabins made ships an unhealthy place for kids. Both of Harriet Allen's children were frequently sick aboard the *Merlin*. Death was not unusual, especially among the very youngest children. Sarah Baker, not yet two, died of dysentery aboard the *Ohio*. Five-month-old Mary Gifford fell ill aboard the *Hope*. Two months later she died while the ship was in the middle of the Pacific. "She had trouble breathing and we could not help her," her mother reported. "We are heartbroken."

HARD CHOICES

For women who wanted to be with their husbands, leaving children at home was not always an option. And those who did leave them home with relatives often regretted it. "I have thought much about my Darling Lizzie," wrote Sarah Cole about her young daughter, "and wished ever so many times she were here with us." Cole's story has a particularly sad ending. Two years into the voyage, she died off the coast of South America and never saw Lizzie again.

Most women and children who sailed on whalers did so only once. Some refused to go again. Others never had another opportunity. Despite the boredom, loneliness, and hardships of being at sea, many women and children never regretted the voyage they made. And a few truly loved their time at sea. "My little cabin never looked better to

These sailing wives posed together in New Bedford, Massachusetts, after long whaling voyages with their husbands.

me than now," wrote Harriet Allen aboard the *Merlin*. "This is my *home*, I have no *other*."

Perhaps in the end, the families who managed to make the whaling ship into a home made the best choice. "I shall feel badly . . . to give up my *Addison* home," wrote Mary Lawrence as her ship approached the end of its journey. "It would be folly to think of spending four years less happily than the last [four] have been spent."

NO MORE WHALES

We will not know for years whether the end of whaling came too late. The "great" whales were all decimated to the point where they may never recover.
                    —Richard Ellis, *Men & Whales,*1991

In the early days of whaling, a reasonably patient captain could find whales nearly anywhere he chose to look. From the North Atlantic to the South Pacific, there was no shortage of whales. While whaling was far from an easy way to make money, the sheer number of whales and the demand for whale products appealed to owners and captains alike. Over time, more and more ships joined the whaling fleet, hoping to cash in on what looked to be a limitless resource.

As more and more whales were killed, however, whalers became victims of their own success. The number of whales worldwide dwindled, and finding prey became increasingly difficult. One by one, the best whaling grounds for sperm whales and right whales were emptied. There are no accurate estimates of the numbers of whales in existence through the nineteenth century, but the decline was clear and dramatic to those who hunted them. In the early 1800s, a New England ship could sail into the North Atlantic and return inside of two years with a full load of oil. In one famous voyage lasting just over a year, for example, Captain Obed Starbuck collected 2,500 barrels of whale oil. Thirteen years later, Starbuck set out again. This time it took him three years to collect half as much oil. By the 1870s, most ships had to sail practically around the world just to find a few whales. Whales were on the path to extinction.

WAR, ICE, AND PETROLEUM

With fewer whales to hunt, the whaling industry became unprofitable. As voyages grew longer and whales harder to find, captains and crews turned to commercial shipping, and owners found other investments. But the decline in the whale population was just one of the reasons for the industry's demise. Three important events dealt serious blows to whaling.

Late in the Civil War (1861–1865), the Confederacy (the South) hoped to wipe out whaling, an industry that mostly benefited the North. The Confederate raider *Shenandoah* headed for the Bering Sea, where it captured or burned about thirty Northern whaling ships. "We have entered into a treaty . . . with the whales," one of the *Shenandoah's* officers said jokingly after scuttling the *Abigail*. "We are here by special agreement to disperse their natural enemies."

Opposite, *Cutting the whale was hard work, but finding whales eventually became even harder.* **Right,** *Captain Obed Starbuck saw his success diminish as whale numbers dwindled.*

A ship that got caught in the ice was in danger of being crushed between the floes.

Dramatic as the *Shenandoah's* voyage was, it was completely unnecessary. Even before the ship arrived in the Arctic, the war had ended. The news simply never reached the raiders. Nevertheless, the raid crippled the Northern whaling fleet. Even under the best of circumstances, it would have taken several years to replace the ships. With the whaling industry in decline, some of the ships never were replaced.

Then, in 1871, ice formed on the Arctic Ocean during a September cold snap. "On the 7th," reported the *Whalemen's Shipping List*, "the *Roman* of New Bedford was drifted bodily out to sea by two floes, and crushed like an egg-shell." The *Roman* was one of thirty-two ships smashed and sunk by the ice. Although the ships were completely destroyed, the crew members all managed to escape on whaleboats. Many barrels of oil and pounds of whale bone were lost. The Confederate attack and the September cold snap destroyed about sixty whaling ships in a span of seven years.

Another big blow to the industry came when scientists discovered petroleum in western Pennsylvania. During the next few decades, more and more petroleum was found. As drilling methods improved, it became clear that whale oil was a fuel of the past. Petroleum was more plentiful, cost less, and was far easier to harvest than whale oil.

MODERN-DAY WHALING

Although a handful of American ships continued to whale well into the twentieth century, they were unusual. U.S. commercial whaling was outlawed in 1971. Only a few nations, notably Norway, continue to hunt whales. Whalers today use high-tech equipment to find their prey. Their weapons are much more destructive than those used by whalers in the 1850s. The hunt is controversial. While some species of whales, such as the minke, are thriving, other species have yet to recover from being hunted almost to extinction during the 1800s. Some scientists and observers argue for looser restrictions on whale hunting, at least for the more numerous species. Others fear for the future numbers of whales if any hunting at all is allowed. The debate is likely to continue well into the present century.

At the same time, a handful of Indian groups have petitioned the U.S. and Canadian governments to allow them to whale. For the most part, these are small northwestern groups that hunted whales before the arrival of Europeans. In great contrast to other modern techniques, these groups usually use the canoes and weapons their ancestors used to attack the whales. They are more interested in reviving cultural traditions than in hunting the whale for food or fuel. This practice, too, is a source of controversy.

Whaling as it existed in the nineteenth century has long since disappeared. But the lifestyle and traditions of the whalers and their families live on in letters, journals, newspaper articles, and the lyrics of old whaling songs. It is these writings, such as the song that follows, that give whaling a human face.

"Blow Ye Winds," traditional whaling song

'Tis advertised in Boston, New York
and Buffalo,
Five hundred brave Americans,
a-whaling for to go.—

Singing, blow, ye winds in the morning,
And blow, ye winds, high-o!
Clear away your running gear,
And blow, ye winds, high-o!

They send you to New Bedford, that
famous whaling port,
And give you to some land-sharks
to board and fit you out.

They tell you of the clipper ships
a-going in and out,
And say you'll take five hundred
sperm before you're six months out.

It's now we're out to sea, my boys,
the wind begins to blow,
One half the watch is sick on deck
and the other half below.

Then comes the running rigging
which you're all supposed to know,
'Tis "Lay aloft" the look-out sights a
school of whales.

"Now clear away the boats, my boys,
and after him we'll travel,
But if you get too near his fluke,
he'll kick you to the devil!"

Now we've got him turned up,
we tow him alongside;
We over with our blubber hooks
and rob him of his hide.

Next comes the stowing down, my
boys, 'twill take both night and day,
And you'll all have fifty cents apiece
on the 190th day.

And when our old ship is full, my
boys, and we don't give a damn,
We'll bend on all our stu'nsails and
sail for Yankeeland.

When we get home, our ship made
fast, and we get through our sailing,
A winding glass around we'll pass
and damn this blubber-whaling.

Anatomy of a Whaling Ship

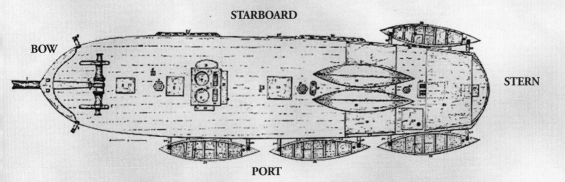

STARBOARD

BOW

STERN

PORT

BOW
the front part of a boat or ship

FORECASTLE
the living quarters of a ship's crew, located beneath the deck in the front part of the ship. The forecastle of a whaling ship is usually extremely cramped.

MAST
the pole that supports the sails

PORT
the left side of the ship

STARBOARD
the right side of the ship

STATEROOM
a captain's quarters aboard his ship

STERN
the rear part of a boat or ship

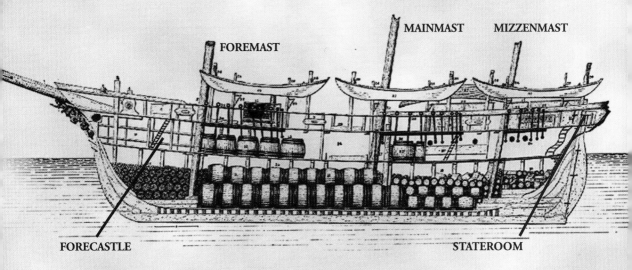

FOREMAST

MAINMAST

MIZZENMAST

FORECASTLE

STATEROOM

WHALING TERMS

ambergris: a waxy, grayish substance found in the stomachs of sperm whales and once used in perfume to make its scent last longer

baleen: the comblike plates of cartilage in a whale's mouth to strain plankton and other food from the water. Also called whalebone, baleen was very valuable for its strength and flexibility.

blanket piece: a long strip of blubber removed from a whale during the cutting in

blubber hook: a large metal hook used during cutting in to pierce the whale's skin

broken voyage: a whaling ship that returns home with less than a full load of oil

crosstree: the part of the ship, near the top of the mast, where the sailor on lookout duty watches for whales

cut in: to cut a whale into pieces and remove the valuable blubber, baleen or whalebone, and ambergris

desert: to leave or abandon a ship without the captain's permission

fin up: dead

flukes: a whale's tail fin

foremast hands: the lowest-ranking sailors on a whaling ship

gally: to frighten (a whale)

gam: to visit or talk with the crew of another whaling ship while at sea

gangplank: a movable bridge used to board or leave a ship

greenhand: an inexperienced sailor making his first whaling voyage

harpooner: a crew member of a whaleboat. Also called a boatsteerer, the harpooner rows in the front of the boat and strikes the whale with the harpoon.

lance: a spearlike weapon used to kill a harpooned whale

landshark: a merchant or supplier who sells overpriced, low-quality goods to crew members of whaling ships

lay: the percentage of a ship's profit that each crew member receives. A sailor's lay usually depends upon his experience and rank.

lookout: the sailor stationed in the crosstree to watch for whales

mutiny: an uprising or rebellion of a ship's crew against the captain

Nantucket sleigh ride: a term used to describe the pulling of a whaleboat by a whale that has been harpooned and is "running"

rigging: the ropes and chains used to control a ship's sails

rig out: to supply a whaling ship crew member with the goods he needs for a whaling voyage

run: to swim very swiftly near the surface of the water. This term is usually used to describe a whale that has been harpooned and is pulling a whaleboat.

salt horse or salt junk: salted beef or pork, preserved in barrels

scurvy: a disease, often suffered by sailors, caused by a lack of vitamin C. Symptoms include tooth loss, weakness, and bleeding.

seize: to tie up a sailor in the rigging as a form of punishment

sound: to dive deep below the surface of the water

span: to come up to the water's surface for air

stove: smashed or broken. This term usually refers to a boat or a ship damaged by a whale.

syndicate: a group of businessmen who own a whaling ship or ships

tradesmen: non-sailors, such as carpenters and cooks, who travel aboard a whaling ship to perform duties other than whaling

SELECTED BIBLIOGRAPHY

Biggins, Patricia. "Doughnuts in the Tryworks: A Child's Life Aboard the *Charles W. Morgan.*" *The Log of Mystic Seaport*, May 1975.

Busch, Britton Cooper. *Whaling Will Never Do for Me.* Lexington, KY: University of Kentucky Press, 1994.

Carrick, Carol. *Whaling Days.* New York: Clarion Books, 1993.

Chase, Owen, et al. *Narratives of the Wreck of the Whale-Ship Essex.* New York: Dover Publications, 1989, reprint of the original 1935 edition.

Creighton, Margaret S. "The Captains' Children: Life in the Adult World of Whaling, 1852–1907." *American Neptune*, July 1978.

Darden, Genevieve M., ed. *My Dear Husband.* New Bedford, MA: Descendants of Whaling Masters, 1974.

Dow, George Francis. *Whale Ships and Whaling.* Salem, MA: Marine Research Society, 1925.

Druett, Joan, ed. *She Was a Sister Sailor: The Whaling Journals of Mary Brewster 1845–1851.* Mystic, CT: Mystic Seaport Museum, 1992.

Ferguson, Robert. *Harpooner: A Four-Year Voyage on the Barque Kathleen, 1880–1884.* Philadelphia: University of Pennsylvania Press, 1936.

Horan, James D., ed. *C.S.S. Shenandoah: The Memoirs of Lieutenant Commander James I. Waddell.* Annapolis, MD: Bluejacket Books, 1996.

Jernigan, M. W., ed. "A Child's Diary on a Whaling Voyage." *New England Quarterly*, vol. II no. 1 (1929).

Lawrence, Mary Chipman. *The Captain's Best Mate: The Journal of Mary Chipman Lawrence on the Whaler "Addison," 1856–1860.*

Edited by Stanton Garner. Providence, RI: Brown University Press, 1966.

Lofstrom, William L. *Paita: Outpost of Empire.* Mystic, CT: Mystic Seaport Museum, 1996.

Morgan, Nathaniel S. *Journal of a Whaling Voyage in the Ship Hannibal*, 1849-50, Log 862. G. W. Blunt White Library, Mystic Seaport Museum, Mystic, CT.

Schmitt, Frederick P. *Mark Well the Whale!* Port Washington, NY: Kennikat Press, 1971.

Stackpole, Edouard A. *The Sea-Hunters: The Great Age of Whaling.* Philadelphia: Lippincott, 1953.

States, John A. *Journal Kept Aboard the Nantasket of New London*, 1845-46, Log 69. G. W. Blunt White Library, Mystic Seaport Museum, Mystic, CT.

Taylor, Nathaniel. *Life on a Whaler.* New London, CT: New London County Historical Society, 1929.

Whiting, Emma Mayhew, and Henry Beetle Hough. *Whaling Wives.* Boston: Houghton Mifflin, 1953.

Williams, Harold, ed. *One Whaling Family.* Boston: Houghton Mifflin, 1964.

FURTHER READING

Baldwin, Robert F. *New England Whaler*. Minneapolis: Lerner Publications Company, 1996.

Carrick, Carol. *Whaling Days*. New York: Clarion Books, 1993.

Chrisp, Peter. *The Whalers*. New York: Thomson Learning, 1995.

George, Jean Craighead. *Water Sky*. New York: Harper & Row, 1987.

Gourley, Catherine. *Hunting Neptune's Giants: True Stories of American Whaling*. Brookfield, CT: Millbrook Press, 1995.

Hall, Daniel Weston. *Arctic Rovings, or, The Adventures of a New Bedford Boy on Sea and Land*. Hamden, CT: Linnet Books, 1992.

McKissack, Patricia C., and Frederick L. McKissack. *Black Hands, White Sails: The Story of African-American Whalers*. New York: Scholastic Press, 1999.

Melville, Herman. *Moby Dick, or, The Whale*. 1851. Reprint, New York: Modern Library, 2000.

Murphy, Jim. *Gone A-Whaling: The Lure of the Sea and the Hunt for the Great Whale*. New York: Clarion Books, 1998.

Roop, Peter, and Connie Roop. *Good-bye for Today: The Diary of a Young Girl at Sea*. New York: Atheneum, 2000.

Author's Acknowledgments

I owe particular thanks to the staffs of the G. W. Blunt White Library at Mystic Seaport in Mystic, Connecticut, and the Old Dartmouth Historical Society in New Bedford, Massachusetts. Thanks also are due to the interlibrary loan department at Adriance Memorial Library, Poughkeepsie, New York, and the volunteers at the Robert Jenkins House in Hudson, New York. The people who work at these libraries and archives were both knowledgeable and helpful—always a good combination.

Thanks also go to Tony Buccelli, Dwight Paine, and Kathy Corrigan of the Poughkeepsie Day School, who not only awarded me a summer grant to help defray some of my travel costs, but also encouraged me to bring whaling into the lower school curriculum.

INDEX

ACKNOWLEDGMENTS

Photographs and illustrations used with permission of: North Wind Picture Archives, pp. 2-3, 9, 23, 37, 46, 49, 53, 59, 62, 71; Corbis-Bettmann, pp. 6, 26, 27, 66, 84; New Bedford Whaling Museum, pp. 7, 10, 12, 17, 18, 34, 40, 50, 56, 81, 82, 87; San Francisco Maritime NHP, p. 11 (G12.21, 599n); Nimrod of the Sea; or, The American Whaleman, Boston, Charles E. Lauriat Co., ©1926, pp. 20, 86; Library of Congress, p. 31 (12453 LCUSZ62 S097); The Kendall Whaling Museum, Sharon, Massachusetts, USA, pp. 45, 68, 77, 78; Brown Brothers, p. 73; Nantucket Historical Association, p. 83.

Front and Back Covers: © Hulton-Deutsch Collection Limited / Corbis